SKILLS FOR SUCCESS

The Essential Resource for Supervisors and Managers

Norco Associates Inc
Toronto, Canada

PRINTED IN CANADA

Editor-in-Chief: D. A. Hollingworth

ISBN 1-896823-10-6

Acknowledgements: We are indebted to the numerous individuals in many different organizations who were willing to share their experience with us. These people have sharpened our understanding of, and insight into, the challenges and demands faced by supervisors and managers today. We appreciate their wisdom, guidance and support. Their influence is found throughout this book.

We are also grateful to the many Human Resources Training and Development Professionals whose ideas and experiences have proved invaluable in shaping the developmental concepts and techniques offered in this book.

Contents

Quality Is Strong Employee Commitment
Building Pride in the Finished Product — The Ten Golden Rules for
     Planning for Quality

5

CUSTOMERS ARE EVERYWHERE — INSIDE and OUTSIDE

External Customers and Internal Customers
Who Are Your Internal Customers?
Customer Issues Should Be at the Centre of Every Major Decision
What Do Customers Want?
Skills, Attitudes and Policies That Win and Keep Customers
Customer Service Is What It's All About

6

MANAGING STRESS at WORK

Stress: What It Is and What It Does
We Need Some Stress to Function Normally
Attitude #1: Taking Control of the Situation
Attitude #2: Getting Involved and Committed
Attitude #3: Letting Stressful Situations Bring Out the Best
Attitude #4: Change and Challenge Can Be Rewarding
Attitude #5: Transforming a Stressful Situation into Something Positive
Minimize Workplace Stress by Managing Your Time
The 24 Hour Countdown Challenge
Ten Tips for Reducing Your Stress Level

7

WORKING WITH a MULTICULTURAL WORKFORCE — DIVERSITY in the WORKPLACE

Communicating Across Differences
Filters — The Elements of Cultural Differences
Language Filters
Tips for Clearer Communicating Across Language Filters
Cultural Diversity in the Workplace
Cultural Value Spectrum
Diversity Is Becoming a Fact of Life

8

TAKING STOCK of YOURSELF and SELF-COACHING

Take Stock of Yourself

The Self-Inquiry Process
Why Is Self-Confidence Important?
Is Your Self-Talk Positive or Negative?
How to Avoid Negative Self-Talk
Keep Your Attitude at Peak Power

9

WHAT ARE YOUR PRIORITIES?
— SET YOUR GOALS and TAKE ACTION

How Often Do You Put Second Things First? — Setting Priorities
Effective Goal-Setting is Key to Success — 6 Guidelines That Really Work
Be Decisive About Your Goals
Stay Focused on Your Goals
Put Self-Motivation in Focus
Inspiring Employees to Meet Their Goals and Give Their Best
Set Your Goals, Achieve Them, and Motivate Others: Motivation Checklist
Do You Receive Respect as a Supervisor?
Motivating Others to Collaborate
The Ten Keys to Really Motivating Your Workgroup
The Power of Praise in the Recognition Process

10

INCREASE PRODUCTIVITY by RELEASING
the POWER WITHIN PEOPLE

How Do Supervisors Lead and Inspire People to Follow Them?
Three Key Personal Characteristics of the Supervisor
Supervisory Leadership Self-Assessment
How Do Supervisors Maximize Commitment?
The Benefits of Fully Committed Employees
The High Costs of Low Employee Commitment

11

MANAGING ANGER and AGGRESSION in the WORKPLACE

How to Deal with an Angry Workgroup Member
Managing Your Own Anger
What to Do When It's You That's Angry
Jealousy and Envy
Violence on the Job
When Personalities Collide

The great overriding objective of learning is not knowledge but action.

CHAPTER 1

Skills for Success : Introduction

Most supervisors and managers understand, regardless of their levels of experience, that people-performance issues are the greatest challenges of their jobs. They also understand that the secret of success in the job lies in being able to multiply their effectiveness through others. As a manager, you simply can't do everything yourself.

Developing sound supervisory skills is the surest path to multiplying your effectiveness through others, and for getting the best from the members of your workgroup. When your employees are productive and performing effectively, you as a supervisor are doing your job.

Skills for Success: The Essential Resource for Supervisors and Managers is designed to cover the key elements for leading and managing people, creating higher levels of commitment, and making the ability to lead others rewarding on a personal level. It is written as an interactive resource to be read easily and understood thoroughly so that the concepts can be readily implemented. The book presents a wealth of "ideas for action" intended for those who want to reach their full potential and make something positive happen in the workplace.

Because it encourages active learning and participation, this book features valuable checklists and questionnaires for determining the overall effectiveness of workgroups and employees alike. These assessment tools provide an indispensable technique for identifying the specific needs of employees. The information gathered from these self-evaluations and questionnaires provides supervisors with an ideal basis on which to establish what changes and improvements must be made.

Strong leadership skills are vital to the workplace as a whole, as well as to each individual workgroup. And these skills can never be underestimated. Each and every employee requires the best level of guidance, support, and motivation possible to enhance quality and production levels.

This resource provides the foundation for understanding what focused supervision and management is all about. It will help you to gain or strengthen the skills that drive employee performance and involvement. This book not only contains valuable insights into these skills, but also into the key strategies that will guide supervisors through the important process of employee achievement by:

> ≫   motivating employees to take on responsibility and perform effectively

> ≫   getting employees to consistently deliver the results you want

> ≫   growing employee capabilities to think and do for themselves

≫ guiding employees to overcome adversity

≫ gaining employee commitment to pride in the finished product.

Skills for Success: The Essential Resource for Supervisors and Managers is written to provide a roadmap for building quality supervisory and leadership excellence. It advances supervisory principles on a practical level and creates a cohesive understanding of the essential elements for effective leadership.

The goal of the book is to empower supervisors to respond to challenges such as workplace stress, staying connected with employees, productivity and performance, and ultimately, developing and retaining the best talent.

The methods and techniques described are a compilation of proven key strategies which are used daily by supervisors in a large number of successful organizations. Some of the major subjects include:

☐ developing your credibility-building actions

☐ minimizing workplace stress — in yourself and others

☐ how supervisors lead and inspire people to follow them

☐ building pride in the finished product — essential steps in planning for quality

☐ the benefits of fully committed employees

☐ managing anger and aggression in the workplace

☐ customers are everywhere — inside and outside

☐ developing the qualities that will help you conquer adversity

☐ being proactive by taking specific action for success

☐ connecting — you know what you're saying, but what are your employees hearing?

☐ taking stock of yourself and self-coaching

☐ the essential ingredients of working with a multicultural workforce

☐ how asking yourself the right questions will help you to reach your objective

☐ using self-evaluation techniques to measure your leadership strengths

☐ essential steps for reducing your stress level

☐ the high costs of low employee commitment

☐ when personalities collide — how to resolve serious differences.

Sound supervisory leadership requires the knowledge necessary to understand the leadership role, the insight to perform the day-to-day activities required of a leader, and a sound foundation upon which to base decisions. It is our sincerest hope that *Skills for Success: The Essential Resource for Supervisors and Managers* will provide that foundation and encourage supervisors to grow personally as they develop their knowledge of successful supervisory techniques.

CHAPTER 2

Action Tools for the Supervisor

Regardless of the organization, industry, or job title, all management shares one mandate — taking action to get things done. If you're a supervisor or manager, you're paid to make sound choices and resolve problems.

This chapter has one simple, overriding objective: to help you improve your supervisory and management skills in order to increase your success. To achieve this goal, you need to learn how to take action. That means developing the ability to analyze situations, choose the best strategy, and implement it.

Possibly, the most critical choices a supervisor makes are those that impact directly on others and the best supervisors try to walk a mile in the shoes of those causing or those affected by a particular problem. They try to view problems from the perspectives of others.

They ask themselves questions such as:

☐ How would I feel if I had to follow these directions?

☐ What does my boss expect from me and why?

☐ How do my workgroup members feel about this situation?

☐ I know exactly what I'm saying but what do my employees hear?

☐ Why do the members of my workgroup act or feel this way?

Successful supervisors solve new and ever-changing problems by taking the right action at the right time. On the other hand, unsuccessful supervisors often fail to act and not only manage by crises, but also continue to wrestle with old problems that they left unresolved in the first place.

By learning to take effective action, you will not only deal decisively with new problems but also decrease the number of old problems that keep resurfacing.

Action Tool #1: Act on It Now!

Adopting an act-on-it-now philosophy will enable you to maximize the performance of your workgroup while making you more efficient in all areas of your life. An act-on-it-now person can always be counted on to get work done on time. These successful individuals avoid putting anything off until later whether it involves taking immediate action, obtaining the facts necessary to make a decision, or thinking things through.

Make the decision to become an act-on-it-now person. This decision may require you to modify some of your work habits. Getting organized, for example, may require a new system for prioritizing actions or implementing a new way for making the best choices.

> By learning to take effective action, you will not only deal decisively with new problems but also decrease the number of old problems that keep resurfacing.

Act-on-it-now people are always specific about what their objectives are. Decide now what your goals and objectives are and begin to separate what you must do to achieve these goals from any other issues that demand your time. Be extremely disciplined with yourself in eliminating any unnecessary work.

Try to become a proactive person who initiates action, instead of a reactive one who needs to be prompted before taking action. Remember though, that becoming proactive and taking effective action is also *a matter of getting your attitude right*.

Action Tool #2: Attitude and Self-Esteem

Successful people develop a "whatever it takes" attitude, and these are the people who are the players in the game of life. They don't just watch life from the sidelines, and they don't avoid risks at all costs. They don't live in fear of making a mistake.

They welcome new issues and challenges with enthusiasm, viewing them as opportunities for growth — both personally and in their work. These individuals tend to get things done and make things happen, and their attitude towards life is usually a constructive, positive one.

An important factor in developing a can-do attitude is healthy self-esteem. People with high self-esteem usually achieve their potential and their goals. They take the necessary risks, they don't wallow in self-blame or self-pity, they trust others and they never remain in the background when they're needed up front.

Evaluate yourself on the Supervisor's Attitude Self-Assessment Profile below. Rate the statements on the four point scale indicated:
3 = Always   2 = More than half the time   1 = Occasionally   0 = Never

Supervisor's Attitude Self-Assessment Profile

1. I feel comfortable when I am set apart from the group.   _____ Points

2. I am able to accept responsibility when things go wrong.   _____ Points

3. I am able to share credit with others.   _____ Points

4. I can accept a compliment without any difficulty.   _____ Points

5. I can envision my goals and *see myself* accomplishing them. _____ Points

6. I feel confident about myself and my abilities.   _____ Points

7. I don't avoid necessary risks at all costs.   ·   _____ Points

8. I think positively whenever I am faced with a challenge.   _____ Points

9. I am able to say "no".   _____ Points

10. I believe the way I react towards people and circumstances _____ Points
    plays a significant role in my happiness and success.

11. I believe people describe me as a positive person.   _____ Points

12. I notice positive qualities first when meeting new people.   _____ Points

13. I am capable of establishing goals for myself and can work _____ Points
    towards them.

14. I view each new situation as an opportunity or challenge.   _____ Points

15. I am able to listen to others.   _____ Points

Total Points _____

Interpreting your score:

38 to 45	*Very high self-esteem. You feel good about yourself and your own capabilities. You are optimistic with a very positive attitude.*
30 to 37	*High self-esteem. You are generally satisfied with yourself and with your capabilities. On an overall scale, you are optimistic with a positive attitude.*
23 to 29	*Moderate self-esteem. You experience periods of self-doubt although you tend to me more positive than negative.*
15 to 22	*Reduced self-esteem. You experience self-doubt at times. You waiver between optimism and pessimism although you are apt to be more negative than positive.*
0 to 14	*Negative self-esteem. You generally do not feel positive about yourself and probably have strong doubts about your capabilities. You tend to be pessimistic and demonstrate negative attitudes.*

Action Tool #3: Build Your Credibility

Do your employees find you credible? Do they trust you? Do they believe in you? Do they willingly follow you? Studies have repeatedly demonstrated the common sense belief that people want leaders they can trust. Similarly, they want leaders who trust them. Honesty and integrity feed trustworthiness because a leader with high integrity is trusted.

When you trust someone or something, you integrate their ideas and their actions with your own. When someone else trusts you, they accept what you and your organization say and do as genuine. Trust, then, is really a choice each of us makes to believe someone or something.

As you build credibility with your internal and external customers, you encourage them to believe that you'll do what you say you'll do. Your internal customers of course, are your fellow workers. Your external customers are those who use your products and services.

When others develop confidence in you and in your company, your repeat business and your word-of-mouth advertising increase exponentially. Employee commitment levels grow as your image becomes internal as well as external. When your organization "walks the walk and talks the talk" by according employees the same high level of respect given to external customers, you build loyalty among all members of your workgroup.

SUPERVISOR TIP

An important factor in developing a can-do attitude is healthy self-esteem. People with high self-esteem usually achieve their potential and their goals. They take the necessary risks, they don't wallow in self-blame or self-pity, they trust others and they never remain in the background when they're needed up front.

Develop Your Credibility-Building Actions. How Would Your Employees Answer if You Asked Them These Questions?

- Do you believe you can be open and up-front with me?

- Do you feel I am truthful with you?

- Do you believe I am good at keeping confidences?

- Do you find I deliver consistent messages in terms of matching my words and deeds?

- Do I keep my promises?

- Do I do what I expect others to do?

- Do you view me as standing up for my beliefs?

- Do you believe that I always have your best interests at heart?

- Do you feel that I consistently "walk my talk"?

- Do you trust that I am as committed to helping you meet your needs as I am about meeting my own needs?

- When you're in a jam, can you count on me to back you up?

Action Tool #4: Avoid These Pitfalls — Things Supervisors Do That Damage Their Credibility

1. Expectations are not clear, or change frequently with minimal explanation.

2. Commitments and promises are made and not kept. The most serious of all.

3. Supervisors favour certain employees: informal or formal power and authority is given to these people.

4. Employees who make *minor* mistakes are subject to unreasonable disciplinary measures.

5. Communication is either infrequent or indirect, and lacks integrity.

6. Conflict is allowed to burrow underground and grow, rather than brought to the surface to be worked through.

7. Reasonable policies, procedures, goals and guidelines are absent.

8. Supervisors avoid making decisions, especially if the decision may not be well received by employees.

9. Supervisors demonstrate an inability to say "no."

10. Supervisors lose their cool in front of others.

Action Tool #5: Overcoming Adversity
— Be Ferociously Persistent

Everyone goes through bad times but successful people know how to snap back. We are all able to persist through the ups and downs we face in our day-to-day lives, as long as we maintain the right attitude and a certain amount of flexibility. We need to develop mental toughness and drive, and focus on what we need to do — not on the obstacles.

We must all learn to be able to brace ourselves for the predictable challenges and setbacks that crop up in all of our lives from day to day. When adversity strikes, as it invariably will, deal with it head on. You can't pretend it doesn't exist, and you can't run from it.

Take immediate action. Accept adversity for what it is, and begin to find ways to confront it. You must strive to become even more positive, because one of the natural by-products of adversity is negativity which will instantly start to creep in. Adversity will usually not resolve itself until you persevere in a positive attitude and begin to take action.

Can You Develop the Qualities That Will Help You to Conquer Adversity?

1. Create a specific action plan for recovery as soon as possible after adversity hits.

2. Commit yourself to an aggressive strategy that will help you triumph over hardship.

3. Remember that every adversity contains within it the seeds of an equal or greater success. Develop the habit of looking for the opportunity that hardship *always* presents.

4. Remind yourself of the occasions when you have previously overcome adversity successfully. Re-live those feelings.

5. Be persistent. Be a survivor. Don't *think*, even for an instant, about quitting.

6. Use this opportunity to prove to yourself that you are in control of your life. Never underestimate your power and ability to push yourself beyond what you're normally capable of. Believe in your power. Believe in your resilience.

7. Get past this disappointment, grief, or anger, so that you can get on with your life. Try to move as quickly as you can through what is sometimes the inevitable period of self-pity or self-blame.

Action Tool #6: Key Steps to Maximizing
Productivity and Performance

Productivity is the efficiency with which we produce products or services. It is a fundamental ingredient in being competitive and hence, is a major contributor to the bottom line. Productivity is an overriding objective in all organizations and supervisors play a key role in productivity improvement programs.

When we hear the word "productivity," we usually think of a workgroup's output in terms of units per shift. But behind this concept of productivity are the people — whether employees, supervisors or managers — who actually perform the actions which generate results.

Supervisors need to apply their skills by using varied approaches to influence employees to cooperate and to be productive. One of those approaches which has proven highly effective is the practice of focusing on changes to production processes inspired by employees rather than managers. This approach offers a diverse and wide range of benefits. Consider some of the advantages of employee input:

■   employees may have more diverse backgrounds than supervisors

- sometimes, employee-based ideas fare better in the game of workplace politics and therefore are more readily accepted by the workforce

- employee suggestions strengthen important team dynamics; after all, you can't do all the work yourself

- employees sometimes have a better feel for how procedures and processes could be improved.

> Trust is really a choice each of us makes to believe someone or something.

Review the Following Questions with Your Team Members to Discover Ideas for Enhancing Performance and Productivity:

☐ is every step in our work process required?

☐ is each step adding value for our customers — both internal and external?

☐ are any steps in the process missing?

☐ are people checking their own work, or does someone else check it when it's completed?

☐ does the work follow a logical flow?

☐ are related processes located next to one another?

☐ are our procedures and policies promoting improvements in performance and productivity?

☐ do we know where the bottlenecks are and how to remove them?

☐ do we allow our employees the latitude and flexibility to make improvements in their own work and work area?

☐ are we able to measure our productivity, to provide us with useful feedback? Do we share it with our workteam members?

☐ to what extent do we encourage our employees to offer ideas and suggestions for improving productivity?

☐ can we identify where the work process stops for the longest time? Do we know why?

Action Tool #7: Decide and Take Action

Good decisions are at the heart of good supervision and management. Our ability to make decisions — to choose between one thing and another, rather than following blind instinct — is a defining feature of our humanity. Whether we work in or with organizations, the quality of our work depends on the quality of our decisions.

How good is your decision making? Do you generally get decisions right, or do you often make poor choices? What factors determine the way you make decisions? On different days, would you make the same decision differently?

You're probably unaware of most of the decisions you make. We make hundreds of decisions every day. Our lives are shaped by decisions, and our success depends on the quality of our decisions and the skill that we bring to making them.

ACTION TIP

All management shares one mandate — taking action to get things done. If you're a supervisor or manager, you're paid to make sound choices and resolve problems.

Making a decision really involves committing to a course of action. It is more than simply choosing what to do. It involves making a rational commitment, however small. As well, it frequently involves making commitments on behalf of others — particularly in a work situation — and asking them to commit to your commitment.

In addition to commitment, a decision always requires action. It includes identifying problems and indeed, the first step in making a decision may be to clarify the issue to be resolved. But again, making a decision always results in action of some kind. This holds true, even if we decide to do nothing, because choosing not to act is as much a decision as any other.

Nothing is more valued in any organization than a good decision. And nothing is criticized more — and remembered longer — than a poorly thought out one. Getting any idea off the ground requires two essential steps. First, you must arrive at a decision. Second, and just as important, you must take action on what you've decided.

Step One: Make the Decision

It's important to understand how decisions are arrived at to learn where you might go wrong. For example, do you tend to cave in under pressure or to be overly conservative? Some supervisors allow themselves to get bogged down in the confusion of having to make rapid choices. But few organizations can afford the luxury of slow management decision making.

Of course, it is your responsibility to gather as many pertinent facts as you possibly can. At some point however, you must make a decision based on your own "gut" feelings. But timing is everything, because even the right decision is wrong if it is made too late.

How much information do you need to make a good decision? It's not practical to put a figure on it but obviously, if you move ahead with only fifty percent of the facts in your possession, the odds are really stacked against you. By the same token though, you'll likely never know one hundred percent of everything you need.

ACTION TIP

Try to become a proactive person who initiates action, instead of a reactive one who needs to be prompted before taking action.

What you must do first is to make sure that the information you do have at your disposal is reliable in terms of where you obtained it. Are the sources trustworthy? Have you obtained feedback and input on the decision by encouraging debate with those whose opinions you trust? Most of all, you must make sure that whatever specific information you do have is clear and makes common sense.

In the final analysis, making good decisions depends on knowing how to take calculated risks. When you don't have all the facts — which is most of the time — asking the right questions can provide you with a powerful approach to speed up decision making and help to reduce the risk.

When you're faced with a variety of choices, what kind of questions can you put to yourself in order to arrive at the best decision?

Asking Yourself the Right Questions
Will Help You Reach Your Objective

A key to reaching wise decisions is to clearly identify and frame the issues so you can make a wise choice. Make a list of all of your options and ask these questions about each of them:

➤ Is this decision necessary? What are the benefits?

➤ What risks are involved?

➤ Must I make a decision now? What happens if I do nothing?

➤ What's the best potential upside I can hope for? What action can I take to maximize the probability of this outcome?

➤ What's the potential downside? Can I handle it?

➤ If this is the wrong decision, do I have a contingency or backup?

➤ Is there any give-and-take in this situation that I should consider? Is there a compromise?

➤ Have I thoroughly examined all possible options to achieve my desired end result? Will I be satisfied with this end result?

➤ What is the most likely result?

Step Two: Take Action

A good decision is of no value unless it's acted upon. Make the decision to act once you have arrived at your decision. But don't forget to set your objectives. Some supervisors are so eager to reach a decision and get moving that they forget to establish a game plan. Consequently, preface every action you take with this question: What are my specific short-term and long-term objectives?

Once you have determined your objectives you can pose the following questions to help you decide what specific action to take:

- what steps must be taken to carry out my objectives?

- how many people will be involved?

- who are the people best suited to meet these objectives?

- to what extent will they require my input and support?

- what resources will they require?

- to ensure cooperation and a successful outcome, should I involve any others?

- what time frame should I allow to complete each segment of my action plan?

- what are the deadlines for each phase of my action plan?

- what mechanisms should I put in place to monitor ongoing progress and get reliable feedback?

- how will I evaluate the long-term effectiveness of my decision?

SUPERVISOR TIP

Supervisors who make progress and get ahead make good decisions and they act on them. That doesn't mean they are perfect, because every decision involves some risk, and no one makes the right decision every time. But evaluating the process in advance by asking probing questions can reduce the risk and turn the odds in your favour.

CHAPTER

3

Do They Understand Your Message?
— Connecting with Your Employees

As a leader, your ability to successfully communicate — to pass on feelings, ideas, experiences and inspiration — allows you to maintain that vital connection with your workgroup. On the other hand, poor communication will always lead to poor performance; yet it is all to common in the workplace.

Fortunately, though, communication skills can be improved; and the better the communication, the better the overall performance and the greater the levels of achievement.

If we want to communicate effectively, we have to be aware of the words we speak and the language we express with our bodies. Good communicators pay attention to the messages they send as well as those they receive. Your communication is effective when someone interprets your message in the way that it was intended.

The better your communication, the more likely you are to achieve your objectives. Effective communication will enhance all the other skills you have to the fullest. The ability to solve problems, motivate, organize, delegate, and obtain information all depend on your ability to communicate successfully with others.

Essentially, communication is a two-way process. In addition to getting your own message across, it is equally important to listen to and understand what others are saying — an approach known as *"active listening"* (see page 3-4). This ensures that you can offer other people what they want, while at the same time, getting the information you need to do your own job.

ACTION TIP

By remaining completely focused on the other person's words rather than on your next thought, *active listening* allows you to effectively evaluate the content of the message. In other words, *active listening* involves demonstrating self-discipline by holding our own ideas, thoughts, and urges to talk.

Communicate to Make the Connection

Supervisors must be able to connect effectively with others if they are to provide good leadership. Leaders must be able to share their ideas and their knowledge to inspire and to transmit a sense of enthusiasm to others. If the supervisor is unable to deliver a message clearly and motivate others to act on it, then no matter how good the message is, it has no value.

Communication is a continuous process, and good communication provides both quantitative and qualitative input. It serves as a yardstick whereby your employees can measure their progress in terms of meeting their goals and objectives.

Here are some things you can do to make sure you connect effectively with others.

☐ Be clear and specific about what you want. Break the task down into step-by-step procedures.

☐ If you're unsure whether or not people have really understood you, have them repeat your message using their own words.

☐ Use demonstrations or illustrations whenever possible.

☐ For more complex tasks, offer instructions for one part of the job at a time.

☐ Use direct, specific language that will be understood. Say exactly what you mean. Don't leave people guessing.

☐ Try not to hurry your instructions. *Good directions save time.*

☐ Avoid misunderstandings by asking employees how they'll approach the issue or task, and why. Have them repeat your instructions when you're finished.

☐ If you're receiving directions or new information, be active. Ask questions. Clarify.

☐ Remain open-minded and patient when you receive instructions from others. Don't second-guess or jump ahead of the person giving directions. Listen to the details.

The Key to Connecting?   ...Start to Really Listen

Good listening skills are the cornerstone of effective communication. We spend about eighty percent of our day communicating from the time we get up in the morning until we go to bed at night — and almost half of that time is spent listening. Yet invariably, the emphasis in business and in schools is placed on teaching people to improve their verbal communication. Consequently, people hear but they often do not listen.

When we simply *hear* someone we can repeat, almost verbatim, what has just been said to us. But we may not understand what was said or even remember it a short while later. However, when we truly *listen* to a person, we focus our attention on what is being said and how it's being said. We demonstrate self-discipline by holding our own ideas, thoughts, and urges to talk. This is called *active listening*.

Sharpening Your Listening Skills

Skilled active listeners send and receive messages effectively, develop better relationships with co-workers, and remember more of what they hear.

Becoming an active listener involves more than just not talking. You have to demonstrate by using the right body language, that the speaker has your full attention. Make sure your active listening skills are effective.

The next time you're involved in a conversation, be aware of the following:

Do I ...

➤ frequently interrupt the speaker?

➤ jump to a conclusion before the conversation is finished?

➤ only pretend to pay attention?

➤ anticipate responses when I ask a question?

➤ avoid facing the speaker and maintaining eye contact?

➤ let my concentration wander from what this person is saying?

➤ show disinterest or boredom by yawning, doodling, or looking at my watch?

➤ find fault with the message?

➤ listen impatiently and act hurried?

➤ allow distractions to divert my attention?

➤ daydream or let my mind wander?

➤ finish sentences for the speaker?

*The more questions you answered with a YES, the LESS you are listening. We may demonstrate poor listening habits because we are tired, preoccupied, distracted **or, we may simply be too busy talking to listen**.*

SUPERVISOR TIP

As a leader, your ability to successfully communicate — to pass on feelings, ideas, experiences and inspiration — allows you to maintain that vital connection with your workgroup.

Nonverbal Messages

Body language is an essential ingredient of clear communication. It is just as important as choosing the correct words. In fact, it may even be more important. Various studies indicate that from 70 to 90 percent of all communication originates from nonverbal sources such as gestures, facial expressions, appearance, posture, use of silence, vocal tone, and inflection.

Using and understanding nonverbal cues can help us to communicate more clearly, credibly, and accurately. Being able to interpret those cues can often tell us what people are really thinking and feeling.

ACTION TIP

Remember one of the most effective forms of body language — a simple smile. A sincere, relaxed smile projects confidence and helps people respond positively to your message.

People are always aware of your actions, and you should understand what body language you use to convey what you are feeling about what you are saying. Practice becoming aware of nonverbal signals: try to notice when you laugh (and why), smile, frown, and raise your voice.

Become conscious of these spontaneous cues and learn to use them effectively in communicating with others. Because so much of what you communicate is accomplished through nonverbal means, you should understand, as a supervisor, that your nonverbal messages will be "read" and understood by people just as readily as your verbal communication.

As we have seen, communication is a series of actions and reactions involving the senders and receivers of messages. It follows therefore, that a good communication process will invariably lead to better job performance — yours and others'. Remember that becoming a good communicator is always an essential means to an end for supervisors who must accomplish most things through others.

Feedback — a Two-Way Process

To be effective, your communication system must be a two-way process. It must provide for feedback. If there is an absence of feedback, you will not know if your message has gotten through and is understood by the other person.

However, the feedback process may not always be as simple as it appears. In some cases, the message is received but not understood, while at other times, it is not received at all. Whether you are giving verbal or written instructions, always make it a point to get feedback to be sure your message has been understood.

Develop the habit of using feedback to determine whether the person really understands what you've said. To get meaningful feedback, make it a practice of noting the verbal and nonverbal reactions to your messages.

If you are to successfully lead a workgroup, it is vital that your members give you feedback. You must be kept informed about how the job is going, how things could be made to work better, and how *you* are performing.

Encouraging the feedback process by two-way communication is really a matter of building trust. If your employees trust you, they will communicate with you openly and often, which will enable you to be a better supervisor.

Feedback Barriers

If we are to successfully send and receive information, it must be a consistent two-way process. However, *feedback barriers* can cause breakdowns in receiving or transmitting this information. These barriers may prevent messages from reaching people thereby making it difficult for the members of the workgroup to effectively perform their tasks.

To be certain individuals understand what is being communicated and the messages are being acted upon, the supervisor must recognize what the barriers are and how to avoid them.

Some of the common barriers to good feedback are:

- ☐ there is no opportunity to offer the feedback

- ☐ the supervisor is not approachable or doesn't encourage feedback

- ☐ fear of disagreeing with the supervisor

- ☐ some workgroup members believe that they are too inexperienced and that their suggestions will not be taken seriously

- ☐ no one asks for feedback

- ☐ the supervisor doesn't seem to listen to the feedback that is offered.

TIP

If the supervisor is unable to deliver a message clearly and motivate others to act on it, then no matter how good the message is, it has no value.

SUPERVISOR TIP

If action is not taken to remove *feedback barriers*, the workgroup's productivity and morale will be diminished, frustration will set in and the group's objectives will not be accomplished.

Has Your Message Been Understood?

There are several factors which affect the way in which we receive feedback. One major factor is the ability to properly interpret feedback so that messages are not misunderstood.

You will become a far more successful communicator when you learn to correctly evaluate and interpret feedback. Some of the most common causes of an inadequate feedback process are:

➤ Biases and prejudices. Are you receiving the feedback with an open mind?

➤ Wrong time for message delivery. Choose the right place and the right time.

➤ Poor listening habits. Are you actively listening and not simply hearing?

➤ Stress. Are you relaxed and open to the feedback?

➤ Wrong method of message delivery. e.g. too aggressive, or sarcastic.

➤ Distractions and interruptions. Are you focused on the person and the feedback? Is your attention being diverted?

➤ Failure to properly interpret the message. Are you receiving the whole message? Remember, the complete message includes not only the words being spoken, but also the person's body language.

When feedback is used effectively it will invariably strengthen the relationship between the supervisor and the workgroup. And your capacity to successfully provide feedback will allow you to maintain that vital connection with your employees. Consequently, always try to consider the following questions before speaking to any member of your group, or to the workgroup as a whole:

- Is my feedback valid?

- Will this feedback solve or create problems?

- Am I presenting the feedback to the right person?

- Is there a risk of harming the workplace relationship by offering this feedback?

- What is the best way to communicate this feedback?

- Is this a suitable time to approach this person or this group?

- Have I chosen the best place to have this discussion?

CHAPTER 4

The Quality Connection — Building Pride

Values and expectations in the workforce are changing and so is the supervisor's role. The supervisor must boost employee commitment and produce a quality product while continuing to fulfil the traditional roles of scheduling work, monitoring progress and leadership.

Quality is a set of requirements, a standard, or a goal. It is about passion and pride. Quality is a measurable goal, not a value sense of goodness. It involves an ongoing effort to improve rather than a set degree of performance. It is always a result. We can only practice quality, we cannot possess it.

In truth, quality is really a performance by which we determine whether we did what we set out to do, when and how we said we would do it, in a way that meets the needs of our customers. In other words, were our customers satisfied with the way in which we made our product or provided our service? If the answer to the question is yes, we can probably say we met our quality goals.

Keys to Delivering a Quality Product or Service

1. Quality Is *Motivated Employee Participation*

Nothing improves relationships with those you supervise more than involving people in the day-to-day objectives of the organization. When those objectives include high standards of quality for products and services, it is essential to foster a spirit of participation, allowing employees to embrace those objectives.

Employee participation, from a supervisory point of view, is not a choice — it is essential. When people feel included, their levels of productivity, motivation, and morale soar. The more input employees have into setting goals and devising their own methods of meeting team and organizational objectives, the more motivated they become.

People seem to perform best when they feel they can contribute to the decisions that affect their work.

When people are fully involved and included as part of a constructive group, they tend to be more energetic, happier, healthier, on time, absent less often, and more productive. Suffice it to say, an improvement in productivity always reflects an improvement on the bottom line.

When individuals have a real sense of involvement with their work and the decisions relating to it, they develop a strong commitment to that work. That commitment frequently translates into a quality product, and trust and loyalty to the supervisor and to the organization.

Remember that people really do want to be involved. And believe it or not, they often have great ideas that will work wonders. Ask them, train them, and give them the right tools. Follow up with quick implementation of their solid ideas to start a steady flow of productivity and quality improvement.

SUPERVISOR TIP

In truth, quality is really a performance by which we determine whether we did what we set out to do, when and how we said we would do it, in a way that meets the needs of our customers.

Tips on Fostering Employee Participation
— Gain Employee Commitment to Quality on the Job

There are a variety of excellent ways to foster employee participation. To promote strong employee involvement, follow these steps:

(a) Find out what parts of their jobs people find the most rewarding. When practical, you can then provide them with opportunities to perform these activities.

(b) We all want to be recognized. Capable employees, quiet employees, gregarious employees and even supervisors need to know that what they are doing is meaningful and important, and is appreciated.

(c) Be enthusiastic. Demonstrate purpose, commitment and inspiration to your employees.

(d) Create an upbeat work environment. Use patience and understanding when working with members of your group.

(e) To the extent that it is possible, nudge employees to take on new responsibilities that are within their capabilities.

(f) Remember, it's not what you say or believe. It's all about what you *do*. So always lead by example.

(g) Be available. Encourage your workgroup to show openness in approaching you with their work-related concerns and suggestions.

(h) Whenever the opportunity arises, be willing to share some of your authority. Try to allow people some latitude in solving problems and in performing their tasks.

(i) If you are able to, include the individuals responsible for meeting the objectives and goals in the process of developing them.

2. Quality Is *High Employee Morale*

It's usually not difficult to spot morale problems in the workplace. Employees become negative and indifferent, with a corresponding drop in productivity levels.

As a rule, the employee with low morale is a dissatisfied and unhappy individual. Because morale problems are contagious, this employee can create cynical feelings and attitudes among others in the workgroup. Because of their potential seriousness, problems of low morale should be dealt with immediately by the supervisor.

Employees with poor morale levels frequently focus on fault-finding, perform their jobs reluctantly, and are often excessively critical of the organization. It is important therefore, to maintain and even enhance a climate that encourages trust, innovation, challenge and employee job satisfaction to keep employee morale high.

When you promote challenge, even timid people become a little bolder and start to look for approaches to overcome the barriers that get in their way. High morale means having a positive and healthy attitude towards the job and the organization. When high morale is present on the team, the quality of their work often *exceeds* the expectations of the supervisor.

3. Quality Is *Strong Employee Commitment*

A strong commitment to quality on the job is really a decision on the part of the employee to follow through on an agreed-upon plan of action. As well, experience shows that employees will be committed to quality to the extent that management is committed.

We are all committed to something, to one degree or another. And generally, our commitments will vary according to our ability to meet them and their relative importance to us. In order for any organization to succeed in its commitment to quality, every employee must demonstrate commitment to quality in every detail.

Commitment to the common goal of a quality product or service is the foundation for all success. It is important to note here that trust directly influences commitment to quality because commitment comes from feeling like a part of the organization and sharing in the organization's objectives.

So important is trust to this process, that an absence of trust will lead not only to a lack of commitment, but also to lower employee satisfaction and a void in meaningful communication.

Commitment and loyalty are always generated from being included, rather than excluded, in decision making and information sharing. Whenever people have a genuine sense of involvement with their job and the decisions relating to it, they develop strong levels of commitment. Invariably, that commitment translates into trust and loyalty, not only to the supervisor but to the organization as a whole.

In your role as supervisor, you must foster the commitment and trust that will be needed to support your efforts at delivering a quality product or service.

Building Pride in the Finished Product
— The 10 Golden Rules of Planning for Quality

You may have observed various quality programs in action at some time in your career. In all likelihood, some have failed, and some have worked. Use the following guidelines to establish a program that will succeed. You can use them to start a new program or improve your current one.

1. Write out and document your plan for inspiring your employees to a quality product or service.

2. Involve everyone you need to successfully carry out your plan.

3. Keep the plan alive by continuously updating it. Fine tune your plan as required.

4. Spread the word. Keep the process conspicuous to everyone involved by posting your action plans.

5. Ask for suggestions. Ask your employees how a process might be modified or how a recurring problem might be avoided to improve quality.

ACTION TIP

Quality is about passion and pride — it is not a value sense of goodness. It involves ongoing commitment to improve rather than a set degree of performance. It is always a result. We can only practice quality, we cannot possess it.

---

6. If necessary, involve those beyond your immediate work area whose support and cooperation you will need.

7. *Stay focused on the specific purpose of your plan*: it is to help you deliver a quality product or service to your customers.

8. Periodically review your action plan to be sure that it fits in with organizational goals.

9. Promote ongoing improvement. At all time, strive to identify and implement improvements which will lead to the goal of consistently producing a quality product.

10. Keep it simple. Remember, quality is always a result. Therefore, we can only practice quality, we cannot possess it.

Supervisors begin the process of becoming quality-focused by setting examples that demonstrate their commitment to a quality product and service. They commit themselves to a process of ongoing improvement and they involve employees in reaching decisions.

Once supervisors have incorporated these principles into their management styles, they can then begin to transfer the principles to their employees.

Developing a quality-focused organization offers real dividends for customers and employees alike. Customers use products and services that offer them the greatest satisfaction — products that not only meet but exceed their expectations. A quality product creates loyal customers who buy more of our products, and make our companies succeed. When companies succeed, it means their employees have secure jobs.

But perhaps even more important, working in a quality-focused organization presents the opportunity to do work that is satisfying and productive; that is, to create products and services that provide meaningful benefits to others. Because, after all, isn't that what we should all want to accomplish in our daily work?

CHAPTER

Customers are Everywhere
— Inside and Outside

There is nothing more important than providing the kind of product and service that creates a new customer or brings an established customer back to your organization. And it is the responsibility of everyone in any company to understand and meet the needs of every customer. Quality customer service is not only a goal; it must be an overriding philosophy that reaches everyone involved in satisfying a customer's needs.

If there is a common denominator shared by all organizations — public or private, large or small, manufacturing, service or government — it is the critical need for exceptional customer service. Good customer service means going beyond the customer's expectations, not just meeting them.

In today's highly competitive marketplace, strong customer service is often the key to remaining profitable and in business. The organizations that understand and foster excellent customer service will be the ones that ultimately both thrive and survive.

Consequently, it is essential to get your people involved in and committed to customer service. Unless your employees see its importance, they may well neglect it through unawareness more than anything else. This is especially true if you supervise a workgroup which doesn't have customers in the traditional sense of the word. For example, if the output of your department is strictly of an internal nature, your employees may not recognize that they have customers.

It is the supervisor's role to educate them continually to the realization that everyone they deal with and serve within the organization is a customer. This is especially critical when the notion of customer service is neither obvious nor ingrained in the corporate philosophy.

External Customers and Internal Customers

There are two basic types of customers:

1. *External customers* are the people we think of as the traditional customer. These are the people that are external to, or outside, your organization. They provide the revenue that supports the company's operations. Without external customers, no one would be in business very long.

2. *Internal customers* are those who work for your company. They may be located somewhere in your building, in another province or country, or even at the next workstation in your department. But if

they depend on you and your work in order to produce their own work, then *they* are your customers.

There is a close and direct relationship between how internal customers are treated and how external customers view the quality of your company's products and services. Generally speaking, an organization's commitment to serve internal customers will unfailingly reveal itself to external customers.

SUPERVISOR TIP

Be sure that everyone in your organization is committed to customer satisfaction. Customers include *external* people — the ones who buy our products and services — as well as those in the supply chain and *internal* people, who are the critical links in the overall chain of achieving customer satisfaction.

Some experts believe that it's virtually impossible to offer high-quality external customer service if a company is not providing good internal customer service. Unless an organization is committed to providing sound internal customer service, service to outside customers will invariably be compromised.

Who Are Your Internal Customers?

External customers are easily identifiable by all of us. External customers are obvious; everyone knows who they are. But internal customers are not so obvious because traditionally we have focused on external customers. For example, Accounting's internal customers may be Production or Marketing or Shipping. In other words, everyone serves other people (internal customers) within the same organization. Everything is a partnership.

Maybe you don't see them every day, or maybe you're not really certain where your work goes when it leaves your department, or maybe the same people you provide service to also provide service to you. *Within your company, your customer is the person who benefits from the work that you perform when it's done well — or alternatively, the person who suffers when your work is done poorly or not at all.*

Once you know who your internal customers are, ask them what they like and what they don't like about the work or service you provide to them. Improve the quality of the work you do by using their feedback. Customers therefore, are really everywhere — inside your company as well as outside.

It is your responsibility to identify your customers, and to know what they need from you and how you can best provide it to them. By doing so, you will optimize both internal and external customer satisfaction.

Customer Issues Should Be at the Centre of Every Major Decision

Successful companies view customers as being at the centre of every decision because customer service is a vital component of success in any business. If your company is to attract and retain customers, your customer service must be better than your competitor's. Experience shows that an organization's greatest profits come from customer loyalty and retention, rather than from the acquisition of new customers.

Customer service pays dividends in many ways, including increased profitability and long-term customer loyalty. Many people understand the cost of acquiring a customer, but not the cost of losing one. In actual fact, it costs five to six times more to find a new customer than it does to keep and do business with an existing one.

ACTION TIP

You should constantly encourage your employees to focus on the importance of meeting customer needs. In a general sense, customer issues should really be the centerpieces of all major decisions.

Forward-thinking organizations provide excellent customer service for three main reasons:

1. ***You gain market share***. When you treat customers well by offering a product or service they desire, they will express loyalty by staying with you and telling others about you.

2. ***You improve the bottom line***. Providing a good product or service profits any organization — public or private.

3. ***It is the foundation for lasting success***. When you offer a quality product or service that your customers desire, make it accessible, and treat your customers well, you are inevitably going to be successful.

What Do Customers Want?

How do you find out what your customers want? To satisfy our customers, it is paramount that we understand what is important to them and then strive at least to meet, if not exceed, those expectations. These needs are not only product and service related. Many factors drive customer satisfaction beyond the core product.

It is important therefore for organizations to develop a solid appreciation for customer needs and expectations. It is only through the process of addressing customer needs that a company produces customer satisfaction. As customers interact with your business they have expectations about several aspects of the interaction and about what is being exchanged. In general, customers really want the following:

1. *A quality product or service.* Simply put, they want to feel they are getting their money's worth, so ask yourself these questions:

   - Where are we not meeting customer expectations for a quality product or service?

   - What are our major competitors doing that we're not doing? How are they meeting customer expectations for a quality product or service?

2. *Availability.* They want to know that they won't have to jump through hoops to obtain your product, so ask yourself these questions:

   - How difficult is it for the customer to obtain our product or service?

   - What do our successful competitors do to make their product or service readily available?

3. ***Quality customer service.*** They want to be treated efficiently and with respect so ask yourself these questions:

    - In what areas do we not meet our customer needs and expectations?

    - What are our main competitors doing that we are not? How are they meeting customer expectations?

    - Where do our processes help or hamper service?

Skills, Attitudes and Policies
That Win and Keep Customers

Problems and customer dissatisfaction can provide the supervisor ideal opportunities for improvement. Always be willing to solve problems by looking at solid long-term solutions, not band-aids. Some organizations make it a practice of asking their customers for criticism and feedback so they can identify problems and nip them in the bud before they arise.

Review the following tips and suggestions to help you and your people provide quality customer service.

- ♦ Constantly encourage your employees to focus on the importance of meeting customer needs. And *good* customer service really means going beyond customer expectations, not just meeting them.

- ♦ Be proactive by seeking out problems. In other words, find them before they find you.

♦ Whenever you can, give your customers choices and allow them to make decisions. Avoid giving them "take-it or leave-it" solutions.

Dissatisfied internal customers will quickly lead to dissatisfied external customers, and dissatisfied external customers will invariably impact your bottom line.

♦ Encourage your customers to visit your workplace. Allow them to provide input on your product and service.

♦ Ask yourself, "What can I offer the customer that they haven't thought of that will add value to this product or service?"

♦ Keep your people up to date and informed on how they're doing in areas such as quality, service, delivery, etc.

♦ Meet customer expectations by being trustworthy and reliable.

♦ Aim high. Quality service can only be meaningfully achieved when each employee feels personally responsible for satisfying each customer — both internal and external.

♦ Remember, the best way to ensure good, consistent service is with happy, motivated employees. Create an upbeat environment by maintaining high levels of morale.

♦ Keep your people informed about what the customer wants — whether internal or external. Your employees should know what these customer needs are and should be trained on how to meet them.

♦ Always keep your word in order to build strong long-term customer relationships.

♦ Increase your customer service awareness by looking at how you're treated by your suppliers. What do you expect as a customer? *What irritates you about doing business with an organization where customer service is a low priority?*

♦ Keep your customers up to date so they can make informed decisions.

♦ Try to think how a customer would think — keep a customer-focused vision.

♦ Always make quality customer service a priority. Demonstrate leadership by getting involved when a customer problem occurs.

♦ Evaluate every step in your process to determine where it could add value to your customer. Eliminate or reduce bottlenecks whenever practical. This will dramatically reduce your delivery time.

♦ Encourage customers to test and evaluate products, services, and ideas.

♦ What is customer service? And who defines it? Our customers decide what it takes to make them satisfied. It is up to you to ask your customers what it takes.

Customers are the lifeblood of any organization; so remember that if you don't take care of your customers, *your competitors will.*

Customer Service Is What It's All About

In essence, customer service is what it's all about, both internally and externally. Without customers, none of us would be in business. Take seriously the idea that your workgroup's job is to support your customers' success.

It really doesn't matter what the workgroup produces, or how large it is, or whether its customers are internal or external. Your group's job is to help your customer succeed — and that is exactly how you and each employee should view it.

How does a workgroup act when it understands this is its job? First and foremost, you, as the supervisor, and every employee realize that you have a genuine contribution to make. But to really support your customers' success, both you and the members of your group must understand what the customer does with what you produce.

You and your employees should also strive to understand how customers' needs are constantly changing and how you can support those changes.

CHAPTER

Managing Stress at Work

Stress is a part of life because today, our lives are complex, and it is virtually impossible to avoid stress. Essentially, stress is what we experience internally in response to a situation we find hard to deal with.

But most of us are able to handle routine stress readily; in other words, we are able to "handle the situation." We are able to dissipate the tension, and resolve our feelings.

Of course, all jobs have their share of stress. If they didn't, they would quickly become boring. So it doesn't matter how much you try to prevent it, some amount of stress in the workplace is natural and inevitable. And organizations must deal with the issue of on-the-job stress, because when employees allow stress to overcome them, they lose their effectiveness — and when employees lose their effectiveness, an organization loses its edge.

Fortunately, you can learn how to manage your stress. While you can't always prevent stress from entering your life, you can take definite steps to reduce the negative effects on your life. Learn how to take control of stress so that it doesn't take control of you.

SUPERVISOR TIP

Feeling that we have control over events in our lives is probably the most important attitude necessary to turn negative stress into positive stress.

Stress: What It Is and What It Does

What does stress mean to you? Is it a traffic jam? Is it missing a deadline? Is it forgetting something important? Is it arguing with someone? Stress is the impact or wear on your body as you experience everyday living. Everyone experiences stress and requires a certain level of stress to function productively. Too much stress though, can have negative effects on your physical, mental, and emotional well-being.

However, what is stressful for one person may not be stressful for another. In this sense, it may be counterproductive to tell someone not to worry about a situation simply because you don't find it stressful. We all react to situations in a different way — it is part of being human.

It is important to remember that stress is not always negative. The goal of stress management is not to remove all stress from your life. Stress in moderation is an excellent motivator and helps you to respond effectively to new situations and challenges. Healthy stress can inspire you and fill you with anticipation and enthusiasm.

We Need Some Stress to Function Normally

Stress, in a sense, is a learning laboratory that constantly gives us feedback about how to successfully handle the challenges we encounter in life. In the same way that regular exercise keeps our bodies physically fit, dealing effectively with the demands in our environment keeps us emotionally fit.

The stress response is basically the same in all of us. The degree to which it affects us depends entirely on how we perceive it and how we handle it. Getting into the habit of viewing stress as something normal and constructive, rather than destructive, is the first step to becoming a healthy and stress-free person.

Stress tolerance begins in our mind and some of us must change our conditioning processes if we are to become more tolerant to stress. There are five basic attitudes that we should try to develop so that stress will work for us instead of against us. By adopting these attitudes on a daily basis, they become part of our normal thinking process and begin to turn our stress into a natural and positive response.

Attitude #1 ...

I feel better about myself when I take control of a situation, rather than letting the situation control me.

Feeling that we have control over events in out lives is probably the most single important attitude necessary to turn negative stress into positive stress. Often negative stress is not caused so much by job pressure, but rather by feeling that situations and events are beyond our personal control.

Once we begin to feel that we're in control of situations, we start to take the initiative and meet them head on instead of sitting back and worrying about how they'll affect us. Eventually, we begin to understand that being in control of situations is much easier and rewarding for us than always being controlled by them.

Attitude #2 ...

Whenever I'm involved and committed, I get a feeling of strength and accomplishment.

Once we become involved or committed to a job, project or activity, we develop a sense of self-worth that's important in how we feel about what we are doing and about ourselves. By becoming committed and actively involved, we develop a purpose and a sense of direction.

Most importantly, we begin to overcome the negative feelings and attitudes that stress creates. By actively participating in situations and events, we develop a better outlook on life and feel much better about ourselves in general. When that happens, we will automatically begin to experience more positives and fewer negatives in our lives.

Attitude #3 ...

Stressful situations bring out the best in me.

We should never deny ourselves the opportunity to be a better person just because we happen to be under pressure or stress. We should try to imagine stress as a battery which energizes us and, without which, we would not be able to reach our full potential.

In fact, some of the best athletes believe that unless they're under pressure, they won't be at their peak. These athletes actually believe that only the stress of competition can bring out their optimal performance. They have conditioned their minds to believe that stress works for them instead of against them.

We all need to become athletes in the sense that our performance will always be better when we're challenged. We'll quickly come to understand how effective stress can be in motivating us to do our very best.

Attitude #4 ...

I find change and/or challenge a rewarding and exciting experience.

Too frequently, we tend to view change in our lives as a negative process. Develop the habit of viewing change or challenge as a rewarding and exciting experience.

The more we practice this, the less threatening change becomes and the more we begin to embrace and welcome change in our lives.

 It doesn't matter how much you try to prevent it, some degree of stress in the workplace is natural and inevitable.

Attitude #5 ...

I can transform any stressful situation into something positive.

There is no reason why we can't think of *something* positive that will result from even the most stressful situation. When we can finally put this belief into practice, we will have overcome a major barrier in becoming stress-resistant!

The belief that we are able to transform something negative into something positive is really a culmination of Attitudes 1 through 4.

In essence, when we become committed and involved, we begin to have a feeling of control over the situations in our lives that make those situations exciting and rewarding experiences.

When that happens, we begin to believe that challenges bring out the best in us and allow us to grow as individuals. With practice and perseverance you'll come to believe that we can turn just about any negative event into a positive experience in our lives.

Integrating these attitudes into our personal belief system enables us to adopt more positive feelings toward stress. The bottom line is that either we allow events to control us or we control and manage them. The choice is ours.

By incorporating the five simple attitudes noted above into our daily lives, we can transform stress into a driving force which enables us to view negative events in a very positive and constructive way.

Minimize Workplace Stress by Managing Your Time

It is well recognized that managing time efficiently is one of the major factors in reducing stress. Often, stress is a result of feeling out of control, either at work or at home, or both.

There are invariably situations which we experience in life that are very stressful. But if we use sound time-management principles and plan what we are going to do, we put focus back into our lives. This enables us to move forward more quickly and return to enjoying life to the fullest.

While you can't always prevent stress from entering your life, you can take definite steps to reduce the negative effects on your life. Learn how to take control of stress so that it doesn't take control of you.

Managing Time

One of the primary causes of stress in the workplace is the feeling that there are just not enough hours in the day to do everything that needs doing. No matter how well we plan our time, there are still only twenty-four hours in a day. When we talk about time management, we are really talking about managing ourselves better and making the most out of each day.

Managing your time doesn't mean cramming more things into an already hectic schedule. It means finding a healthy balance between your work life and your personal life — between the things that you *have* to do and those things that you *want* to do.

To make the best use of your time and minimize stress, you need to manage each day carefully by employing sound time management techniques. There are really two sides to good time management: things we want to do and things we want to avoid doing.

For example, we might want to:

➤ use time at work more effectively

➤ get more things done in the available time

➤ feel more relaxed and in control of our time

➤ set realistic goals and priorities

➤ effectively manage distractions and interruptions.

Some of the things we might want to avoid:

☐ procrastinating

☐ rushing to meet deadlines

☐ feeling stressed and out of control

☐ being late for meetings

☐ wasting time

☐ forgetting to do important things.

Many of us feel threatened or driven by time. We become anxious about tight deadlines, we are overwhelmed by urgent tasks piling up, and we are under increasing pressure to improve our skills and produce better results.

Other people seem to be able to use time as if it is a resource like any other. Because they know what their priorities are they're able to plan the best way to allocate their time. These people remain calm and in control, even when unexpected events threaten to send them temporarily off course. The best time managers are those who have developed a sense of different kinds of time, namely:

(i) the time that they must plan, use and control in the most efficient possible way, and

(ii) the time during which they are free from the pressure of time.

Are you controlling your time or is it controlling you? Are you able to change your approach to time, depending on what you are doing? In general, the way you manage your time reflects your attitude to life. Accepting that you are in control of your life and assuming responsibility for the way in which you use your time is the first step to a constructive attitude.

One thing is certain. Once you begin to effectively use your time, you will soon notice significant improvements in all other aspects of your life.

The 24-Hour Countdown Challenge

The moment you get up, your clock starts ticking. Today, you have a million and one things to accomplish! Will you be able to squeeze them all into one day? Is it possible for you to accomplish all the things you have planned?

Do you know how to best organize and balance your available time and your tasks? Try this quiz at the end of the day, and judge for yourself how you did.

DID I ...

♦ handle interruptions and distractions well?	☐ yes	☐ no
♦ remain focused on the job at hand?	☐ yes	☐ no
♦ delegate all that I could delegate today?	☐ yes	☐ no
♦ prepare a daily "to-do" list?	☐ yes	☐ no
♦ avoid procrastinating and not put things off for another day (i.e. did I do what I set out to do today)?	☐ yes	☐ no
♦ set realistic goals and priorities that I could achieve today?	☐ yes	☐ no
♦ evaluate my progress several times during the day against my "to-do" list?	☐ yes	☐ no
♦ avoid "managing by crisis" today?	☐ yes	☐ no
♦ use waiting time to get things done?	☐ yes	☐ no
♦ make good use of my break times to re-energize myself?	☐ yes	☐ no
♦ eat properly and manage to get a good night's rest?	☐ yes	☐ no
♦ avoid "time-wasters" and take steps to eliminate them?	☐ yes	☐ no

Ten Tips for Reducing Your Stress Level

1. ***Be flexible enough to change***. By being flexible in the way we approach problems we may find a better way of organizing our lives and achieving our objectives. We should always have the courage and the wisdom to do things a better way.

2. ***Talk to yourself in a positive way***. Whenever we find ourselves in the midst of a stressful situation, we should take a minute to find something positive in the event. The worse possible thing we can do is say something negative to ourselves.

3. ***Avoid perfection***. Another common stress-inducer is our desire to be perfect. No matter what your goal, you won't be perfect one hundred percent of the time. In other words, the result may not be perfect, but is it acceptable?

4. ***Don't live in the past***. We can only live in the present and, perhaps the future, but we can't do anything about the past. Instead of dwelling on the past, take a moment to view past experiences in a positive way in terms of what you learned from them.

5. ***Visualize positive results***. When we're in stressful circumstances, it is common with some of us, to visualize the worst that we expect to happen. Instead, take a second or two to think about a good result. In other words, *expect a successful outcome.*

6. ***Create quiet time alone — everyday***. It may be before you go to work or after you arrive home, but you may need no more than half an hour a day to read or listen to music or do nothing at all. Don't be

frightened of your own good company. Alone with your thoughts, you'll get to know yourself again, and in the process reduce your level of stress.

7. ***Reward your successes and accomplishments***. Don't just check your accomplishments off your list, recognize them and acknowledge them — and the talent, energy, and perseverance they required.

ACTION TIP

The stress response is basically the same in all of us. The degree to which it affects us depends entirely on how we perceive it and how we handle it. Getting into the habit of viewing stress as something normal and constructive, rather than destructive, is the first step to becoming a healthy and stress-free person.

8. ***Keep a healthy lifestyle***. Watch what you eat and drink, and exercise regularly. Regular exercise is considered one of the best ways to relieve anxiety and tension. It invigorates and energizes us — physically, mentally, and emotionally.

9. ***Build confidence to reduce stress***. When you start new tasks, remember the times when you have been successful in the past to build your confidence. Accept negative feelings as part of the process of change. Confidence is the ability to lift yourself above those feelings, past mistakes and failures.

10. ***Develop an expectant, winning attitude***. What we expect in life usually becomes reality so expect the best for yourself always. Stay positive.

One final note on managing stress — don't take yourself too seriously. Look for humour and enjoy it often. Humour and laughter are often the elixirs of life. Did you know that every time you laugh, your brain releases substances called endorphins which relieve your body from its pain and discomfort?

Laughter is contagious and indeed powerful in its overall effect. Have you ever found yourself in a tense and difficult situation when suddenly someone cracks a joke, laughs or giggles, and all the tension instantaneously evaporates, as everyone "breaks up" with laughter? Immediately, communications improve and dialogue becomes easier as people lower their guard and relax in their common humanness.

Laughter is powerful magic! Are you laughing enough? If not, allow yourself the best dose of medicine available to all of us — "laughter."

Especially, lighten up a bit and learn to laugh at yourself. It'll improve your immunity to stress.

CHAPTER 7

Working With a Multicultural Workforce — Diversity in the Workplace

Each year, the Canadian work force becomes more diverse. In just about every company, you will find a broader range of ethnic groups and nationalities than ever before. There are also more older workers, people with disabilities, and workers with just about every conceivable personality.

The multicultural makeup of organizations has changed and with it the diversity of languages. For an individual whose homeland is different from our own, the transition can often be quite challenging as new environments, languages and customs are experienced. Employees within this group require encouragement and support to help them in their transition.

It is true that employees will often bring with them talents and expertise in many fields, but they may experience difficulty in applying those skills due to language and cultural filters. This factor can contribute to difficulty in expressing themselves or, in some cases, understanding spoken messages.

Communicating Across Differences

While many people talk, fewer people communicate. Communication involves the process of reaching understanding; it results in the creation of shared meaning. When co-workers of different cultures communicate, they tend to strengthen relationships and learn to understand one another better. Unfortunately, misunderstandings can occur when they *don't* communicate.

Communication doesn't happen by itself. It requires effort, especially when communicating with someone of a different culture. That's because people of different cultures have different communication styles and values, which you have to grasp before you can understand the true meaning being conveyed.

It is important to remember that our cultural backgrounds have considerable impact on how we say things, how we hear things, and how we interpret what we see and hear. It is culture that determines the topics we feel are suitable for discussion at work, how direct or indirect our statements are, and whether we make or avoid eye contact.

Filters — the Elements of Cultural Differences

In many cultures, communication is more than just words; it involves the entire context of the encounter. The status of the individuals, body language, voice tone, the setting, and phrasing all contribute to the subtleties of what is being expressed. The exchange of information is usually subordinate to building and maintaining the relationship.

North Americans for example depend on verbal and linguistic communication. On the other hand, people of other cultures may use innuendos and non-verbal communication to allow people to maintain their dignity in awkward situations.

The elements that make up these cultural differences are called *filters*. Consequently, if your workplace includes people with generational or cultural differences, realize that you may encounter filters in communication.

Language Filters

Obstacles which may prevent messages from reaching the other person are often referred to as "filters" or screens.

You may have employees in your workgroup who speak a different language than the one being used. These individuals may sometimes tend to hear your words in their own language, and while they may be fluent enough to carry on a light conversation, they are sometimes limited to an extent that we don't fully appreciate.

ACTION TIP

Diversity is no longer a matter of enlightened social policy. It is becoming a necessity. There are simply not enough talented people available for any organization to cut itself off from any potential pool of applicants.

It is important to remember that the English language can be difficult to master since there are many different meanings for commonly used words. To address this difficulty, the supervisor must be aware of any language filters his or her team members may experience. When verbal or written filters of this type are encountered, the supervisor should use easy-to-understand dialogue and refrain from using complex words or statements.

If the necessary resources are not available within the organization, guidance and training can be obtained through outside sources to help an employee through this transitional process.

High self-esteem plays a vital role in the way people react towards others and their ability to successfully cope with everyday problems including language difficulties. Self-esteem is essential to every employee who is to succeed on the job. Suffice it to say that these people require ongoing motivation, support and encouragement to maintain that self-esteem and to reach their full potential.

Tips for Clearer Communicating Across Language Filters

- speak clearly and precisely

- condense your communication to the main point

- refrain from elaborate explanations; they can be confusing

- avoid the use of slang expressions

- watch for non-verbal clues instead of asking, "Do you understand?"

- reiterate your main point

- use a short, written message or visual material when appropriate

■ speak simply, but use correct English

■ communicate what you want done and how to do it to promote employee productivity.

Cultural Diversity in the Workplace

As a rule, until people have the opportunity to learn otherwise, they assume that other people look at the world just as they do. They think everyone has similar values and everyone is motivated for the same reasons. They don't question their assumptions, they believe that's just the way the world is.

SUPERVISOR TIP

The more we learn about, understand, and become sensitive to the differences amongst people, the better we are able to motivate them.

The behaviours we've absorbed since our childhoods reflect differences in societal values and behaviours based on how and where we were raised.

Some of the factors affecting these differences are:

☐ traditional family behaviours and values in the home, which are influenced by race, gender, religious beliefs, education, etc.

☐ individual idiosyncrasies and personalities

☐ where you were born, what region within that country, what city — urban or rural, and what particular neighbourhood.

Today's workforce is truly a mosaic of different ethnic groups, religions, races, genders, and ages. As the supervisor, your job is to ensure that divergent pieces of the mosaic fit together in a coordinated way, fully utilizing the abilities and talents of each employee.

When skillfully managed, this diversity can bring to an organization a competitive advantage. However, if it is not properly managed, it can negatively affect the bottom line and the work environment can become un-welcoming.

Diversity is challenging, yes, but it's also richer, livelier, more fun and ultimately more profitable. The members of any organization should recognize and understand that diversity is a business issue that affects their ability to compete.

As new technologies make the world smaller and smaller, our diversity puts us at the forefront of a new international order. If an organization doesn't accept the realities of diversity, and teach employees how to thrive in a diverse culture, how will it fit into the global economy?

Cultural Value Spectrum

One of the ways to understand differences in the various cultural styles is to compare the different value systems commonly held throughout the world. While this information is non-specific, you can use it as a general comparison to see how significantly people from one culture can differ from people of another. Once you are aware that such divergences exist, you'll be better equipped to understand and lead people from diverse cultures.

Remember that there is no right or wrong position on the spectrum of values. Individuals in any cultural group will vary in terms of their values and their beliefs — there is no top or bottom to a values spectrum. Spectrums indicate a continuum rather than fixed movement from left to right or good to bad.

Cultural Value Spectrum

formal approach	informal approach
group oriented	individual oriented
cooperation	competition
emphasis on long term	emphasis on short term
people-related emphasis	task-related emphasis
fluid view of time	controlled view of time
open and accessible	personal privacy
authority/order	equality
indirect style of communication	direct style of communication
continuity emphasis	change emphasis
reserved personality	outgoing personality
avoid confrontation and conflict	non-averse to confrontation
emphasis on preparation and planning	emphasis on action
conservative approach	risk-taking approach

Diversity Is Becoming a Fact of Life

Diversity is no longer a matter of enlightened social policy. It is becoming a necessity. There are simply not enough talented people available for any organization to cut itself off from any potential pool of applicants. Promoting the concept of a diverse workforce provides an organization with the best chance of remaining competitive.

In order to make workplace diversity a success, the supervisor should commit to:

➤ providing ongoing training/development and ongoing support

➤ creating models of suitable behaviour within the organization

➤ recognizing and respecting others and their individuality

➤ understanding the inherent value of having a diverse workteam

➤ leading by example.

It bears repeating here that we should not accept diversity solely because it's the politically correct thing to do. It is a business decision.

We must remember there are some facts about the workplace which are unavoidable. First, it will become increasingly diverse not increasingly similar, because of increasing global markets and demographics. Second, such diversity is an inherent benefit not an inherent threat because it enlarges and strengths the mosaic. And third, organizations which resist diversity will dilute their energy and time on activities which are not geared toward customers, success, and the bottom line.

CHAPTER

Taking Stock of Yourself and Self-Coaching

Good self-coaching is the most successful route for multiplying your effectiveness as a supervisor. The ability to coach yourself begins with taking stock of your strengths and weaknesses, and it can take you from where you are to where you want to be. Asking searching questions and giving yourself constructive feedback will encourage you to become more aware of your true potential.

It's a process that helps you to build on your strengths and to develop new skills, so that you can take on new challenges. A sound approach to self-coaching enables successful supervisors to learn from both their successes and their mistakes. As their competence and confidence improve, their self-esteem grows and they are able to express their potential to the fullest.

Take Stock of Yourself

Self-coaching involves being able to pinpoint and remove barriers to your own improved performance. It means asking yourself good questions and giving honest answers. A sound approach to self-coaching focuses on the here and now, not on yesterday's mistakes.

To identify insights into your particular situation, you engage in a process of self-inquiry. You're not necessarily looking for the quick answer here, you may sometimes need to look more deeply than that, by asking yourself a broader range of questions.

The Self-Inquiry Process

Here are some examples of questions that you may want to use in the self-inquiry process:

- ☐ What am I trying to achieve?

- ☐ Why is that important to me?

- ☐ How will I know when I have succeeded?

- ☐ What is preventing me from achieving this?

- ☐ What am I tolerating that I could change?

- ☐ What different ways can I use to get there?

- ☐ What is the one thing I could do right now that would make a difference in moving toward what I want to accomplish?

- ☐ What resources are available to me that I'm not using?

- ☐ Are there any biases or self-limiting beliefs that are holding me back?

- ☐ What am I not doing?

- ☐ Am I moving toward or away from my objective?

- ☐ In order to achieve what I want, will I have to give up anything?

- ☐ Do I have any concerns about what others might say about me?

- ☐ How would achieving what I want allow me to move forward?

- ☐ Are there any actions that I'm afraid to take, and why?

- ☐ What am I overlooking?

- ☐ Am I being truthful to myself?

 Successful supervisors understand that today's actions are always guided by tomorrow's needs, not yesterday's habits.

Once you have completed the self-enquiry process, it requires commitment on your part to follow through on your answers to the questions above. Without commitment, any change you're intending to make is less likely to occur.

When you begin to gain insight into some of the beliefs that may be limiting you, you also begin to see new options and possibilities. But without commitment, you will remain forever in the "thinking about the options" stage.

*Whereas a goal sets a specific direction, **a commitment** involves a pledge to a course of action which you make to yourself.* Whatever it is you wish to accomplish will only happen after you make a clear commitment followed by actions to support it.

Why Is Self-Confidence Important?

As a rule, the best supervisors are self-confident enough to reassure others and appear in control. And, of course, it is important to remember that strengthening and developing your self-confidence is always the basis for improving your supervisory leadership.

Self-confidence and leadership feed upon each other. When people perceive you as a self-confident person, they are more likely to accept you as a leader. As people grow to accept you as a leader, your self-confidence is boosted.

It is the supervisor's responsibility to ensure strong performance from his or her employees, meet goals, stay on top of things, and be prepared for contingencies. Invariably however, along the way, supervisors will run into problems and obstacles with both people and things.

On those difficult occasions, striving to meet goals successfully may elicit feelings of doubt in one's ability to reach those goals. The only way to manage that doubt is to affirm your own self-confidence. In the process of doing this, you will be encouraged to adopt a positive frame of mind and to follow through.

Develop the ability to believe in yourself and to persevere. Together, belief in oneself and perseverance form a potent combination; they are the keys to personal and career success.

Self-confidence is measured in a number of ways. And when it comes to self-confidence, successful supervisors consistently demonstrate certain traits which are indicated on the checklist that follows. How many of these traits have you developed?

The best leaders display their self-confidence by . . .

- ▸ sharing their goals and expectations with others

- ▸ being willing to confront people and situations when necessary

- ▸ saying "no" when they have to

- ▸ enjoying challenges rather than avoiding them

- ▸ being willing to openly share their knowledge and expertise

- ▸ persevering and following through

- ▸ not being easily overwhelmed by people or circumstances

- ▸ being able to make decisions and seeing them through

- ▸ making it a habit to read books or listen to tapes on leadership, motivation, inspiration, goal attainment, and perseverance.

SUPERVISOR TIP

Develop the ability to believe in yourself and to persevere. Together, belief in oneself and perseverance form a potent combination; they are the keys to personal and career success.

Is Your Self-Talk Positive or Negative?

In order to project a strong leadership image and to be self-confident, positive self-talk must replace negative self-talk. Positive self-talk means saying positive things about yourself to yourself. And without boasting, positive self-talkers also make positive statements about themselves when speaking to others.

We can help to make our self-talk positive by developing a healthy attitude. A person's attitude is their way of thinking, and to a large measure your attitude will determine how well you do your job. A change in attitude will always reflect a corresponding change in your level of self-confidence.

Bear in mind that the most highly valued trait in the eyes of many organizations is a positive, "can do" attitude. If you want your employees to have a positive attitude and excel, you must be willing to set the example. You must demonstrate the positive attitude you want your people to have all the time you are around them.

ACTION TIP

The High Expectancy Success Theory generates effective results for many individuals. This theory states that the more you *expect* from a situation, the more *success* you will realize. However, remember that this theory cuts both ways — if you expect failure, you increase the chance of encountering failure.

But simply talking about positive attitudes won't work — you must always lead by example. At the end of the day, it's really up to you. The supervisor's ultimate goal is to create an employee attitude of, "Whatever I'm doing, I'm going to do the best job I can."

How to Avoid Negative Self-Talk

The other side of developing a healthy attitude with positive self-talk is to avoid negative self-talk. Minimize negative statements about yourself to others to boost your self-confidence. That way, you'll appear more like the leader you want to be.

You create what you see in your mind. More often than not, what you think about is what you get. Your objective should always be to eliminate negative self-talk by maintaining an inspired outlook that rejects the language and the thoughts that hold you back.

Try these suggestions:

- Instead of saying "I'll try," say "I will." The phrase "I'll try" can sometimes imply "I really don't want to do it, but I feel compelled to do it."

- Learn to graciously accept praise and compliments instead of feeling that you're not worthy of them. Simply respond with a big "thank you" and nothing else.

- Eliminate the *could's, should's, have to's,* and *ought's.* Using these words tends to increase your guilt and your stress. For example, instead of saying "I should conduct a coaching session tomorrow," say "I will conduct a coaching session tomorrow."

- Never say, *even to yourself,* "I'm too (disorganized, weak, afraid) to..."

- Develop the ability to comfortably accept offers of help from others instead of habitually responding with a "No thanks, I can handle it myself."

■ Don't mumble. Speak confidently, clearly and distinctly.

■ When people ask you how you're feeling (even if it's simply routine), reply "Great" or "Wonderful," but not just "Okay" or "Not bad."

Keep Your Attitude at Peak Power

Attitude is a mind-set, and a successful attitude is all in your head. To a large extent, it's determined by your powerful thoughts.

If these thoughts are positive and directed to the future, they'll help you achieve your highest objectives.

But if, on the other hand, they are negative and mired in the past, they'll sap your energy and stall your growth and development. Lurking in the back of your mind, they can sometimes be behind problems like procrastination, low self-confidence, poor time management, and a general lack of direction.

SUPERVISOR TIP

Self-coaching involves being able to pinpoint and remove barriers to your own improved performance. It means asking yourself good questions and giving honest answers.

A sound approach to self-coaching focuses on the here and now, not on yesterday's mistakes.

Here are some tips on how you can keep your attitude at peak power:

☐ Focus only on what you can control — yourself. Always take responsibility for your problems. If you blame others, it will rob you of control over your own life.

☐ Turn negative situations into favourable ones by making a list of all the positive aspects of what might seem to be adversity.

ACTION TIP

Self-confidence and leadership feed upon each other. When people perceive you as a self-confident person, they are more likely to accept you as a leader. As people grow to accept you as a leader, your self-confidence is boosted.

☐ Don't apologize for your ideas ("This may not be a great idea, but...") Get use to stating your proposals and opinions assertively and boldly ("I can find a way to do that.")

☐ Take a few minutes to vividly imagine what it would be like if you achieved all your goals. How will you feel? Where will you be? What will you be doing? How will you solve your problems? Let that vision guide your actions and your thoughts. Act like the person in that picture.

☐ Identify and deal with one negative habit at a time. With daily effort, it takes from two to four weeks to develop new positive thought habits.

☐ In addition to leading others, you must always be your own leader. Know who you are, where you're going, and what you want. Trust yourself and be confident about your informed decisions.

☐ Devote fifteen or twenty minutes each evening in reviewing the day's events. What did you do well? What might you have done differently? What can you change tomorrow?

☐ Allow yourself to make mistakes. Everyone makes mistakes and so will you. Learn from them. Never dwell on past mistakes; that creates a negative self-image.

SUPERVISOR TIP

*Whereas a goal sets a specific direction, **a commitment** involves a pledge to a course of action which you make to yourself.* Whatever it is you wish to accomplish will only happen after you make a clear commitment followed by actions to support it.

☐ Try to surround yourself with people who are positive and up-beat, are supportive of your career goals, and have the characteristics you want to develop.

CHAPTER

What Are Your Priorities?
— Set Your Goals and Take Action

Your effectiveness as a supervisor will be determined by your ability to establish your priorities as you progress toward your goals. With many activities and responsibilities demanding your attention, you need a way to determine which goals receive the investment of your energy and your time. Only with an effective method for setting priorities will you be able to concentrate on the tasks for reaching your goals.

By setting priorities you can learn to apply your time and energy to high-priority issues. Once you are have set your priorities, decisions are more easily reached. When demands are made on you, you can decide how much time to allocate to a particular request. You can actually develop habits that will help you get work done and achieve your goals. Learning to set your priorities means knowing how you are going to use your time and that your decisions will bring you closer to achieving your goals.

How Often Do You Put Second Things First?
— Setting Priorities

Take a few minutes to respond to the following checklist for setting priorities.

Checklist for Setting Priorities

Do I ...

1. regularly set priorities? ☐ yes ☐ no

2. use a consistent standard for determining my priorities? ☐ yes ☐ no

3. understand the importance of applying my energy and my time to high-priority issues? ☐ yes ☐ no

4. determine priorities on a short-term basis as well as on a long-term basis? ☐ yes ☐ no

5. communicate my priorities to those individuals who are affected by my actions? ☐ yes ☐ no

6. consistently work on what I have determined are my high-priority issues? ☐ yes ☐ no

The question, "If you don't know where you are going, how will you know when you get there?" makes a lot of sense. Few people would set out on a journey without knowing where they're heading. Yet this is what many of us do in our lives, with the result that we often drift aimlessly, wondering why it is that we feel frustrated and stressed out. We are often so busy that we don't have time to stop and think why we are not achieving what we want to achieve.

As a supervisor, before you can effectively set your priorities you need to be quite sure of two things:

(i)   what you are actually doing with your time; and

(ii) how you want to be spending your time once your priorities are set.

There are three primary areas that can distract us from focusing on and establishing our priorities:

1. ***Responding to the demands that others place on us.***
    In your case, it may be your colleagues, your workteam, your customers, or your suppliers. If you include family and friends to the list of other people that make demands on you, the list starts to look frighteningly long. If you try to meet all of these demands, you will lose sight of what it is you want to accomplish.

2. ***Spending our lives dealing with crises and problems.***
    Some supervisors run from one crisis to another — finding last minute replacement for staff who are ill, dealing with equipment that is broken down, pacifying angry customers, resolving conflicts between team members. But if you spend all of your time picking up the pieces when things have gone wrong, you can't focus on the more positive aspects of your job. When you start to establish your priorities — planning ahead — you will be able to avoid the pitfalls of management by crises.

3. ***Doing things out of habit.***
    Habits are routines or repeated patterns of behaviour. And human beings are creatures of habit. But if we get used to doing too many things out of habit, without thinking about *why* we are doing them, or whether we should be doing them at all, we will not be successful in setting our priorities. The key is to be sure that your habits are helpful and productive rather than the contrary.

Effective Goal-Setting is the Key to Success — Six Guidelines That Really Work

1. ***Effective goals are written.***
    Many of us daydream about the things we would like to accomplish. But before we can achieve those dreams we must pick up a pen and write down the things that we most want to achieve. Once your goal is committed to paper, it becomes concrete. When you write out a goal, you give it life. You actually see what you're thinking. You have a target to aim for ... something that takes shape and grows legs. Your goal is no longer just a dream, it has now been given a sense of reality. Writing down your goals is always the first step toward achieving them. Goals not written down fall victim to the "out of sight ... out of mind" phenomenon!

2. ***Effective goals are written in specific, measurable terms.***
    When you are specific in writing your goals, you have probably expressed them in a clear, measurable way. In other words, goals must be easily definable and measurable so that your progress toward them can be monitored and evaluated, and so that you'll know when you have achieved them.

3. *Effective goals are attainable.*
   Good goals should require you to stretch a bit in order to challenge your skills and abilities. The real trick is to make the goal realistic enough so that it is reasonably attainable without discouraging your effort and performance. As your success and confidence grow, you may then decide to stretch for a higher goal.

SUPERVISOR TIP

Always establish the best goals you can. Goals are the seeds of success — you become only what you plant.

4. *Effective goals are manageable.*
   On occasion, a goal may seem overwhelming because of its scope but if you divide that goal into smaller components, it becomes easier to manage and is therefore more achievable.

5. *Effective goals can be visualized.*
   Practice picturing yourself reaching your goal. Feel the end result, the moment, and your emotions. Most of the energy that drives us to reach our goals comes from our desire to attain them. In general, the stronger and more focused your desire, the more quickly you will achieve your goal.

6. *Effective goals require periodic evaluation of your progress.*
   A periodic review of your goals will go a long way in ensuring that they continue to be timely, realistic and well-defined. A regular, *honest* evaluation of your progress increases the probability of reaching your goal.

Be Decisive About Your Goals

The fundamental difference between what one individual and another achieves is determined more by goal choices than by ability. The major differences between successful people and others are in the goals they choose to pursue. *People with similar abilities, talents, and intelligence will achieve noticeably different results because they select and pursue different goals.*

Never overlook the obvious; the nature and direction of your life will change the moment you decide *what* goals you want to pursue.

Stay Focused on Your Goals

Focus generates a powerful force — goal power. The instant you focus on a goal, it becomes a magnet which pulls you and your resources toward it. The more you focus your energy on your goal, the more power you generate. There is an exponential increase in performance that takes place when you stay focused on your goals.

Stay focused. Resolve not to be distracted. Without focus, your goals become faded aspirations ... enthusiasm dissipates ... and you lose your way.

Put Self-Motivation in Focus

Motivation is the spark, the enthusiasm, the drive, that propels you into action. Motivation involves the desire to achieve a goal and the willingness to take the necessary actions to accomplish that goal. Without motivation, goals become unattainable and you lose touch with your own power and potential. Although motivation must come from within, others can inspire you and you can also inspire others.

What is self-motivation? It is the innate ability to summon, without outside influence, the inspiration to tackle challenging assignments and to do them to the best of your ability. Self-motivated people don't see themselves as powerless, and they don't make excuses. They don't wallow in self-pity or play the "blame game" for their situations. Self-motivated people focus on their goals and accept full responsibility for achieving them.

SUPERVISOR TIP

Without a game plan and purposeful action, the only guarantee is mediocrity and perhaps, failure.

Inspiring Employees to Give Their Best

As a supervisor, you probably already recognize the importance of employee motivation. You also likely understand that an absence of employee motivation can significantly affect your company's productivity. At best, motivation problems keep your workgroup from reaching its full potential. At worst, they can put your workgroup's future in jeopardy.

Motivation is a curious thing. Sometimes, supervisors may have a difficult time describing it, but they never have a problem figuring out when it's absent — employees become bored with their jobs, the quality of products and services drops, creativity takes a nose dive, productivity goes down, careless mistakes increase.

But how exactly do we define motivation? Typically, a motivated workplace would include some of the following:

- ■ *Low employee turnover*. Motivated employees feel good about their jobs and their company and are exceptionally loyal to their employers. As a rule, they are less likely to leave if the company goes through a difficult period or to experience the "grass-is-greener" syndrome.

- ■ *Open information flow*. Employees feel motivated when they know what's going on. They aren't blind-sided with unexpected information. In turn, they don't mislead their managers or conceal information. There is mutual respect, whereby both sides listen to one another and provide feedback. Also with open communication, grapevines tend to wither because there are better, more reliable sources of information readily available.

Motivation is a curious thing. Sometimes, supervisors may have a difficult time describing it, but they never have a problem figuring out when it's absent.

- ■ *Strong customer service, both externally and internally*. Employees are committed to providing the best service they can, helping internal customers (their co-workers) as well as their external customers. While they may never interact directly with outside customers, highly motivated employees understand that they can impact customer satisfaction by doing their jobs well.

- ■ ***Responsibility for actions and commitment to results***. Every employee strives to do his or her best and is committed to the overall success of the organization. By understanding how their particular roles fit into the bigger picture, motivated employees are able to make decisions and take responsibility for their actions.

SUPERVISOR TIP

At best, motivation problems keep your workgroup from reaching its full potential. At worst, they can put your workgroup's future in jeopardy.

- ■ ***Lively interaction***. Active, lively collaboration among employees is another hallmark of a motivated workplace. Rather than trying to out-do their co-workers or toiling away in isolation, motivated employees enjoy cooperating with one another and working in productive groups.

- ■ ***Ingenuity and creativity***. People feel motivated when they're encouraged to experiment with approaches they themselves developed and when they know they can be part of a solution. This sense of ownership fosters a creative, dynamic atmosphere in which employees take the initiative in clever, original ways.

Set Your Goals, Achieve Them, and Motivate Others

Remember, as a supervisor your major responsibility is to keep your workgroup focused and motivated. Review the following motivation checklist summary to help you achieve those goals.

Motivation Checklist Summary

<u>Do</u>	<u>Don't</u>
Focus on strengths and natural talents.	Focus on weaknesses or shortcomings.
Be fair and consistent in your treatment of employees.	Play favourites.
Offer others encouragement.	Underestimate others.
Give and encourage honest feedback.	Blame others.
Be honest and direct.	Try to manipulate others.
Recognize the efforts of others.	Insist things are always done your way.
Discover the needs of other people.	Go back on your word.

Do You Receive Respect as a Supervisor?
Become a Great Motivator.

Gain respect as a motivator. It's one thing to be given the mantle of leadership — it's another to have those whom you supervise feel you deserve it. Follow the examples of some of the great motivators and you can increase the respect you receive as a leader and supervisor.

Great motivators *earn trust*. Be honest with people. Your word must be the most valuable thing you own.

Great motivators *serve*. You should be more concerned about the welfare of your people than you are about yourself. Ask, "How did I motivate my employees today? What did I do for them? How did I encourage their efforts? Did I give them what they need in order for them to give me what I want?"

Great motivators *are humble*. Give more credit and recognition to your employees than they expect. Sometimes, be willing to accept more blame than you deserve. Maintain humility.

Great motivators *have vision*. They dream do-able dreams. Decide where you want to go, put it in writing, and get enthused about it. Include something in your game plan to excite the people around you and then share the vision.

Great motivators *enjoy what they do*. Supervision isn't a punishment. Don't be afraid to drop your guard and laugh at yourself. Strive to create an environment where smiles generate all the light that is needed to get the job done.

Great motivators *listen*. Encourage your employees to share their frustrations, their aspirations, their worries and their desires. Ask them what ideas they have for achieving your vision.

Motivating Others to Cooperate and Collaborate

The importance of cooperation and collaboration in motivating employees cannot be overstated. A well-organized group should always produce better work than individuals working alone towards the same goal. It simply amounts to the concept of *synergy*, where the whole is greater than the sum of its parts. An efficient workgroup should always produce better results, more consistently, than if unconnected people were to toil on the same project.

The other great benefit of synergy is that it inspires employees by giving them a feeling of belonging — something they may not be getting elsewhere. If you've ever been part of a really successful workgroup, you know the good feelings you get from working together to do the best job you can.

SUPERVISOR TIP

The bottom line is that employees thrive on recognition and supervisors who fail to realize this fact are depriving themselves and their workgroup of a powerful form of inspiration to shape desired performance and behaviour.

Whether the workgroup is a small business working toward an organizational objective or a small team within a production department, the group needs to have a goal.

Whatever the goal is, everyone needs to buy into it. It needs to be more important than individual agendas. In other words, personal recognition should always be secondary to attaining the group's objectives.

Ultimately, it is the responsibility of the supervisor to ensure that all group members embrace the common goal, because that is what motivates the group and holds it together, and allows it to continue when times are tough. Your role as supervisor is to keep the group focused and together and foster a winning team spirit.

Carefully Consider the Ten Keys to Really Motivating Your Workgroup

1. Always treat workgroup members fairly and with consideration and respect.

2. Offer support to group members in their efforts to meet team goals.

3. Understand each member's abilities and provide assignments based on these abilities.

4. Be accessible. Listen actively without interrupting.

5. Make sure each person knows they are an integral member of the group.

6. Offer credit and recognition for a job well done.

7. Provide clear direction that is readily understood and accepted.

8. Keep workgroup members enthused and challenged by their work.

9. Show genuine interest in each person as an individual.

10. Encourage workgroup members to make decisions related to their jobs.

ACTION TIP

The major differences between successful people and others are in the goals they choose to pursue. *People with similar abilities, talents, and intelligence will achieve noticeably different results because they select and pursue different goals.*

The Power of Recognition in Motivating Employees

It is impossible to overemphasize the importance of appealing to the recognition needs of others to spur them on to higher levels of productivity. Recognition efforts must always be honest and genuine. Making people feel important is also essential to gaining their support for you as a leader. Your work as a supervisor is unfinished until you satisfy an individual's need for recognition.

Many factors traditionally considered motivators by conventional wisdom are now viewed instead simply as "satisfiers". For example, money, benefits and working conditions are important factors in keeping employees satisfied but they have proven not to motivate many people beyond a certain level of achievement. However, some of the factors that are consistently shown to be strong motivators are:

- [ ] opportunity for growth

- [ ] recognition of a person's individuality

- [ ] praise for accomplishments to stimulate further achievements

- [ ] challenge and job satisfaction — the strongest of all job motivators.

Praise Plays a Vital Role in the Recognition Process

Praise is vital in motivating people but it doesn't always work. Some supervisors praise every minor activity, diminishing the value of praise for real accomplishments. Others deliver praise in such a way that it seems insincere. Try these suggestions to make your praise more meaningful:

Be specific about the reason for your praise. Instead of saying, "Good job!" It's much better to say, "The information you gave me on our scheduling problems really helped me to understand the issues involved."

Don't overdo praise. Too much praise diminishes its benefit. If it's overdone, it loses its value all together and may seem insincere and automatic.

Praise must be meaningful. Avoid the practice of simply recognizing peoples' accomplishments in passing. Instead, offer to spend some time with them so that they know their efforts to the organization and to the workgroup are recognized.

Be sincere. Don't try to fake sincerity. You must genuinely believe that what you're praising an employee for is commendable. If you don't believe it yourself, neither will the employee. A sincere thank-you means a lot. You can hand out a dozen job-well-done trophies but unless you make the recipient feel that the recognition is heartfelt, you're not truly recognizing the individual. In fact, cookie-cutter thank-you approaches may even harm your relationships.

Don't be afraid to publicize praise. While reprimands should always be given in private, praise, whenever possible, should be given in public.

More often than not, it is fitting to allow your entire workgroup in on the praise. When other team members are aware of the praise you give an employee, it spurs them to work for similar recognition.

Make it immediate. Recognition is always most effective when it comes as soon as possible after the desired achievement or activity has occurred. Saving your praise for a later time will lessen its impact.

ACTION TIP

> Making people feel important is essential to gaining their support for you as a leader. Your work as a supervisor is unfinished until you satisfy an individual's need for recognition.

Recognize to improve performance. Recognizing strong performance is an excellent way to inspire employees to improve in weak areas. Never offer recognition for ordinary performance. When you praise people for doing routine jobs, in a routine way, you're not inspiring them to do better, and it will make the recognition you give them for outstanding accomplishments seem less important.

Supervisors must understand that employees want to know if they are improving and performing in their jobs — and delivering direct, simple recognition for a job well done is the most effective way to provide that recognition. The bottom line is that employees thrive on recognition and supervisors who fail to realize this fact are depriving themselves and their workgroup of a powerful form of inspiration to shape desired performance and behaviour.

CHAPTER

10

Increase Productivity by Releasing the Power Within People

As a leader, your job is to provide members of your workgroup with the fuel that will "start their engines" and keep them going. Not all engines, of course, take the same kind of fuel to keep them running and so it is with people. What works for one person may not motivate another.

To be successful in keeping your team moving forward, you have to know what kind of fuel to feed each of your members, how and when to use it. For the supervisor, it can be a challenging task, but it's more than worth the effort.

Good supervisory leadership requires the ability to make things happen by channeling and encouraging the contributions of others. While it is true that some people appear to be born leaders, anyone can learn what effective leaders do and how to apply these skills to themselves. To become an inspiring leader you must know yourself, your particular situation, and your team.

Remember that with leadership, your supervisory abilities will come to life — without it, your abilities and talents will remain hidden and you will have only marginal influence on others. You must understand that in your role as supervisor, you should always be ready to be the inspirational force behind your team, thereby leading it forward to success.

How Do Supervisors Lead and Inspire People to Follow Them?

As a supervisor, you will be successful — that is, you will have people follow you — only when people *think* they are making a difference, *feel* they are making a contribution, and *know* that their efforts are being recognized. To make this happen, you must embrace four basic principles. Once you have done this, your people will know what is expected of them and where they can make a difference.

They will also know how they will benefit from their commitment to making a difference. Successful supervisory leadership demands much from the supervisor but the rewards — both personal and professional — for you, and for the work team, are substantial. Below are these critical principles:

1. ***Drive and enthusiasm***. It is hard to think of an effective leader who is not enthusiastic. It is almost always the enthusiasm of the leader that provides the basis for the workgroup's inspiration. Could you ever see yourself motivated by someone who is indifferent to whether a task gets done or not? Strong leaders are driven by a desire to achieve that goes beyond money or status. Their motivation is internal, a part of themselves, and not built on external factors such as position, personal power or money considerations.

Drive and enthusiasm also involve commitment and determination. Leaders must be able to take a positive view of things, even when they go wrong, thereby demonstrating that problems can always be overcome. Good leaders set high standards for themselves and put their energy into raising their performance beyond generally accepted levels.

SUPERVISOR TIP

Effective supervisors always understand the value of employees and their vital role in achieving company objectives. And they strive to help their employees tap into energy, power and initiative that they didn't know they had.

2. ***Honesty and integrity***. Above all, a leader must always act with honesty and integrity. These two qualities are the foundation of trust between the leader and members of the team. Without trust, your efforts to lead are doomed to failure.

   Honesty and integrity mean being trustworthy and open, and matching your words with your deeds. Your integrity establishes the rules by which you treat others and demonstrates your values. Survey after survey reveals that individuals claim the quality they look for and admire most in their leaders is integrity and trust.

3. ***Self-awareness and self-confidence***. These are the keys of sound leadership and involve the ability to honestly understand your own strengths and weaknesses. They include humility (i.e. recognizing that you

have weaknesses), ability to admit your mistakes, confidence in your strengths, and a good grasp of how you need to improve.

This requires you to show consistency in your attitudes and in your actions. Acting exclusively on your own feelings may lead you to be unfair and inconsistent.

Just a word on self-confidence here: you needn't be an extrovert to be a leader or to be self-confident. However, you must have the belief and confidence that you will ultimately succeed in what you are doing, and be able to effectively transmit this confidence to others.

As a leader, your job is to provide members of your workgroup with the fuel that will "start their engines" and keep them going. That fuel is inspiration.

4. ***Working relationships***. A good leader develops the social skills to establish relationships quickly by establishing a rapport, not only with the workgroup but with all people with whom he or she comes into contact. Building this rapport requires a willingness to show a sincere interest in other people and to seek common ground so that progress can be made. Sometimes leaders need to learn how to build networks in order to foster an atmosphere where things can be achieved more quickly.

In addition to dealing with conflict and finding solutions to both long and short-term problems, an effective leader's ability to find common ground and build on it is critical in managing working relationships.

Three Key Personal Characteristics of the Supervisor

There are countless, different leadership and supervisory styles. But whatever the style, a strong leader must possess and continually develop the following three personal qualities, each of which is equally important and complements the others:

1. *Competence*. For supervisors to maintain the trust and cooperation of their workgroups, they must possess suitable expertise in their fields. However, remember that technical know-how does not necessarily translate into competence. Competence must also include such factors as following through on commitments, managing time effectively, and sometimes dealing with customers. However, a deficiency in technical knowledge can often be overcome by strong supervisory management abilities.

2. *Personality*. Competence may give you the authority to lead others but only for a limited time. Because without the right personality, you'll eventually lose the attention and respect of your workers. Consequently, it is worth noting that a friendly, engaging and sincere personality will lead people to trust you, to believe in you, and ultimately, to follow you. In other words, if you get along, they'll go along.

3. *Empathy*. Genuineness and sincerity are paramount. Your workgroup will grow wary of you if they sense there is a lack of substance behind your charming personality. Empathize with your workers by letting them know that "we are all in the same boat." Let them know that the outcome of a project has the same level of importance for *everyone* involved.

Always be fair and honest. In order to maintain your ability to lead, influence, and persuade others to follow you, you must be known for your fairness, and above all you must be known as trustworthy.

Supervisory Leadership Self-Assessment

You should have an idea of how strong your supervisory leadership skills are at the moment so that you can focus on those areas that need the most improvement. By completing the Leadership Self-Assessment Questionnaire which follows, you'll be able to more easily identify some of your strengths and weaknesses, and put your own skills improvement program in place.

	Always	Sometimes	Rarely
Goals and Planning			
1. For every task, I set realistic, measurable and specific objectives.	☐	☐	☐
2. When the workgroup has been given a task, I allow time to plan for completion of the task.	☐	☐	☐
3. I make it a point to have a contingency or "back-up" plan in the event that problems occur.	☐	☐	☐
4. When faced with a problem, I evaluate different solutions rather than jumping to a conclusion.	☐	☐	☐
5. I estimate how long a job will take before giving it to my workgroup.	☐	☐	☐
Listening and Feedback			
1. I spend as much time listening as I do talking in my dialogue with team members.	☐	☐	☐
2. I communicate regularly with the workgroup to brief them and to get their input.	☐	☐	☐
3. Team members approach me with ideas on how to improve individual or team performance.	☐	☐	☐
4. I ask my workgroup members how I can help them work more effectively.	☐	☐	☐
5. I invite input from the team on my performance.	☐	☐	☐

Prioritizing and Time Management

1. I prepare a daily "to do" list. ☐ ☐ ☐
2. I assign maximum priority to ideas and suggestions that help to achieve our workgroup goals. ☐ ☐ ☐
3. In order to know what I should be doing, and when, I plan my time in advance. ☐ ☐ ☐
4. I perform the tasks that I cannot delegate. However I delegate the tasks that others in the group can do. ☐ ☐ ☐
5. I *prioritize* each job on my "to do" list. ☐ ☐ ☐

Inspiring Team Members to Action

1. When it's deserved, I give recognition and praise to group members for a job that is well done. ☐ ☐ ☐
2. I make it a point to interact and speak with each team member, each day. ☐ ☐ ☐
3. I employ varied approaches to motivate and inspire different members of the group. ☐ ☐ ☐
4. Whenever possible, I offer people a challenging task and the opportunity to develop through their job. ☐ ☐ ☐
5. I try to match jobs to individual personalities to maximize their motivation as members of the group. ☐ ☐ ☐

Larger Goals — Meeting the Organization's Objectives

1. I make it a point to remain in touch with my organization's vision and goals. ☐ ☐ ☐
2. I foster a vision within our team that matches the objectives of the organization. ☐ ☐ ☐
3. I monitor the team to be certain that it is meeting the needs of our customers and clients. ☐ ☐ ☐
4. I encourage the workgroup to contribute to accomplishing our objectives and our vision. ☐ ☐ ☐
5. I make team members aware of how their roles fit in with organizational goals. ☐ ☐ ☐

How Do Supervisors Maximize Commitment?

A workgroup, a department or a project will stand or fall on whether or not its members are fully committed to its success. Your challenge as a supervisor is to obtain that commitment, not from just one person but from the whole team or, quite often, from the whole department.

Effective supervisors always understand the value of employees and their vital role in achieving company objectives. And they strive to help their employees tap into energy, power and initiative that they didn't know they had.

SUPERVISOR TIP

For all their differences, employees in general, agree on one thing. They feel best about themselves and their work when they are emotionally committed to the company they work for. They view commitment as a high priority.

The Benefits of Fully Committed Employees

When employees are *fully committed*, everyone wins. Here's how:

- **Strong Morale**. When employees are committed, they enjoy their work. Not only do they love their jobs, there are fewer accidents, less illness and absenteeism, less conflict and more fun, and in general, the workplace atmosphere is positive and upbeat.

- ***Strong Performance Levels***. When people are committed to their jobs, they care about the organization's goals, objectives and vision. They are more apt to give the extra effort required to increase production and performance levels.

- ***High Quality Product or Service***. When employees are committed, they care about the quality of the goods or services that the organization provides. They are enthusiastic and eager to offer creative suggestions on how to improve services or products. It should also be remembered that a company which embraces high quality standards is more likely to attract talented workers who are seeking employment with an organization they can be proud of.

- ***Minimal Turnover Rates***. Workers who are committed to the company, and feel, in turn, that the company is committed to them are far less likely to leave their jobs. There are noticeable decreases in turnover and absenteeism. In fact, it is not uncommon for committed employees to value their existing job relationships so highly that they even pass over more financially lucrative opportunities to go elsewhere.

ACTION TIP

Above all, a leader must always act with honesty and integrity. These two qualities are the foundation of trust between the leader and members of the team. Without trust, your efforts to lead are doomed to failure.

- *Fosters Team Spirit*. Employees with high levels of commitment buy in to the organization's objectives and vision and there is a greater sense of cooperation and group collaboration. Team members are more likely to readily work together as they bond with one another. A team spirit naturally evolves when individuals are committed to their co-workers and to the company.

- *Creates a Workplace Which Attracts Desirable, New Employees*. Most people want to work in an organization with a reputation for good morale, high team spirit, low employee turnover. They want to enjoy their jobs, bond with their fellow workers and feel committed to their organization.

  When organizations understand this need, they will tend to attract the most talented individuals from a shrinking pool of skilled workers.

The High Cost of Low Employee Commitment

When employee commitment is low, supervisors and management will observe some or all of the following manifestations:

- ☐ *Weak Morale*. Without commitment, employees are less likely to enjoy their work. Workplace accidents and absenteeism tend to increase as do stress-related illnesses. In general, the overall atmosphere of the workplace suffers and becomes negative.

- ☐ *Weak Performance Levels*. As commitment drops, employees are more apt to be satisfied with doing the minimum. In other words, they often do just enough to keep their jobs. The company's objectives seem remote and distant to them.

☐ ***Poor Quality Product or Service***. As commitment slides, employee concern about the quality of goods and services diminishes. Employees are cautious and tend to avoid any risk, thereby withholding their ideas and suggestions for needed improvements. Invariably, quality suffers.

SUPERVISOR TIP

You must understand that in your role as supervisor, you should always be ready to be the inspirational force behind the team, thereby leading it forward to success.

☐ ***High Turnover Rates***. When commitment is absent, people tend to leave the company at the first sign of trouble.

☐ ***No Team Spirit***. When commitment levels drop, an attitude of "everyone for themselves" prevails. People withdraw from productive collaboration with each other and become obsessed with protecting their own turf or special interests. They develop feelings of isolation and separation, not only from each other but also from the organization.

☐ ***Creates a Workplace Which May Repel New Employees***. Because commitment and morale are vital to most individuals, potential employees will tend to seek out organizations that foster an atmosphere of mutual trust and loyalty. Companies and organizations who do not respond to this need in potential new employees, will ultimately lose the competition for new, desirable workers.

A final word on the vital importance of commitment and trust.

Commitment and trust are inseparable! As the foundation for success, building trust with your employees and customers will create loyalty, lower turnover, repeat business, and excellent word-of-mouth advertising.

But the concept of trust may, at first glance, seem too abstract to be an effective business strategy. More and more successful organizations, however, are recognizing the value of building commitment and trust among employees and customers as an essential process to improving the bottom line.

CHAPTER

11

Managing Anger and Aggression in the Workplace

Because anger is a natural emotion, it would be unrealistic to ask people never to feel it. Instead, the goal is to help — and sometimes *insist* — that at work, they deal with their anger less aggressively and more appropriately. Anger in the workplace interferes with performance, productivity, and quality. It also creates an environment that is negative, hostile, and sometimes frightening.

People do really want to get along at work. Very few individuals want or desire conflict. To the contrary, most people greatly prefer harmony to conflict, and a sense of peace to feelings of anger. After all, people come to the workplace to work — not to quarrel.

Excessive conflict and anger at work will only bring out the worst in everyone, leaving them drained of energy and demoralized. A reasonable amount of conflict in the workplace is inevitable, given the reality of individual personalities with their many varying needs and wants.

Occasional conflict, on the one hand, is to be expected, and if it's well-handled, can build trust and increase cooperation. And it is noteworthy that people often emerge from *constructively* handled conflicts with an improved sense of effectiveness and self-esteem.

The goal of this chapter is to help supervisors understand how to manage workplace conflict and anger — their own, and others'.

SUPERVISOR TIP

Keep communicating. Many people avoid conflict by withdrawal of one type or another. Remember that the longer you maintain open communication, the greater the chance that the issue will be satisfactorily resolved.

How to Deal With an Angry Workgroup Member

People experience a spectrum of emotions all the time, from annoyance to outright anger. Like conflict, sometimes anger can be positive if it focuses a person's energy to overcome obstacles

But when it is directed at an individual, it can invariably be destructive.

Here are some strategies the supervisor may wish to employ to deal more effectively with the angry person.

☐ **Listen, by allowing the person to be frustrated or angry**. Let them vent.

☐ **Don't personalize**. Any comments directed at you should not be taken personally. Avoiding overreaction to the situation will allow you to maintain control. When your own emotions are in control, people who are frustrated or upset can be dealt with in a positive and constructive manner.

☐ **Watch your words**. Avoid language that might provoke further anger.

☐ **Control the situation**. Speak in a calm tone and maintain a quiet, calm posture. Raised voices only fuel anger and frustration, and accomplish nothing.

☐ **Let them finish**. Allow them to get things off their chests.

ACTION TIP

Admit that no one can make you angry; *you* get angry. You are the only person who is in control of your emotions. You injure yourself by relinquishing that control to others.

☐ **Show concern**. Strong emotions are often a natural reaction to a difficult situation. Your job is to clarify the problem the person is facing and help him or her deal with it. Try to confirm your understanding with the issues either verbally or by nodding agreement.

☐ **Pinpoint the problem**. Try to understand what the person is attempting to convey. Ask occasional questions but allow them to do most of the talking. When they have finished, provide feedback by briefly summarizing your understanding of what they have said. Once the problem is clarified, help the person deal with it so it does not recur.

☐ **Use "I" instead of "you."** People who are upset sometimes react unfavourably when confronted with "you" statements. Try phrasing your statements using "I" messages. For example, rather than saying, "Why did *you* do that?"; say, "*I* need help in understanding this situation..."

Managing Your Own Anger

There is no denying it: sometimes, difficult situations and difficult people can make us all angry. Anger is often a natural, but usually unproductive emotion in dealing with a difficult personality. Unfortunately, however, too much anger at work destroys the morale of the workgroup, lowers efficiency and causes a variety of other problems.

Experts suggest taking a more thoughtful approach to our anger. They believe that we should take responsibility for our anger instead of claiming that we just can't control it.

Taking personal responsibility for our behaviour instead of blaming situations or blaming others can be difficult. But if we persevere, the payoff is getting more done on the job, feeling better at work, and taking less stress home at the end of the day.

What to Do When It's You That's Angry

Here are some practical ideas about what you can do to manage your own strong emotions.

- Find the trigger. When does frustration, anger, impatience or another strong emotion rear its head? Do you associate it with a particular individual, time of day, or subject?

- Identify what made you angry. Did someone hit one of your "hot buttons"? What feelings or perceptions did you arrive at that triggered your anger? Are they valid?

TIP

Occasional conflict is to be expected, and if it's well-handled, can build trust and increase cooperation.

- Recognize that an angry exchange of words changes few minds. Neither side is listening well enough for this to happen.

- Act, don't react. Begin responding to people and stop reacting to them. Focus on events, actions and things, not on the individual.

- Admit that no one can make you angry; *you* get angry. You are the only person who is in control of your emotions. You injure yourself by relinquishing that control to others.

- Try the old count-to-ten technique. The idea here is to create a buffer time to allow your emotions to cool off.

- Strive to remain polite. Social rules like proper manners and civility help us manage anger because they force us to maintain respect for others.

- Try to understand why you are using your anger. For example, is it being used to: (a) correct the situation? (b) prevent recurrence? (c) communicate feelings of hurt or disappointment?

SUPERVISOR TIP

If you frequently feel angry, keep an anger diary. Note what triggers your anger: when, where, with whom, its duration, the intensity, and how you expressed it. What patterns do you observe?

- Learn to notice your anger warning signs, such as a racing heart or tightness in your stomach. Train yourself to take preventive action when you feel these changes.

- Learn to be an observer in your own life. Objectively view what happens to you. Evaluate your responses. Commit to doing better next time.

- Keep communicating. Many people avoid conflict by withdrawal of one type or another. Remember that the longer you maintain open communication, the greater the chance that the issue will be satisfactorily resolved.

Jealousy and Envy

Jealousy and envy often follow when employees perceive there is favouritism shown for particular people. Jealousy is an inevitable byproduct when employees believe praise, rewards, or recognition is based on favouritism rather than on accomplishment of the task itself. Jealousy and envy can foster lower productivity and morale problems along with resentment.

When individuals are working in a team environment, it is sometimes a challenge for the supervisor to accurately assess respective performance levels. Supervisors must therefore, to the best of their ability, always be objective in offering recognition and praise.

Sometimes, it is advantageous to allow the workgroup as a whole to share in the recognition of a job well done. This approach eliminates repeatedly praising the same employees while ignoring the efforts and achievement of those who have not yet reached higher levels of performance.

Jealousy and envy can be effectively minimized when everyone is treated fairly on a consistent basis. This goal is best accomplished when the supervisor strives to give equal recognition to every member of the workgroup.

It is noteworthy that people often emerge from *constructively* handled conflicts with an improved sense of effectiveness and self-esteem.

Violence on the Job

While most workplaces are considered to be protected and safe, violence on the job can occur with potentially harmful consequences for the employees involved. A growing number of organizations are developing an understanding of the factors that contribute to violence and are putting programs in place that deter violent behaviour.

Events that could eventually lead to violence are described by experts in the field as "critical incidents." These include:

- ☐ verbal threats to harm co-workers

- ☐ refusal to follow company policy

- ☐ physical intimidation

- ☐ demonstrating hostility and antagonistic behaviour to co-workers

- ☐ threats to damage company property.

Sometimes, unfortunately, these events are minimized, ignored or dismissed. It is vital, however, that they are recognized as warning signs to be addressed promptly and effectively.

Some companies operate with the belief that "It could never happen here." But taking this approach can leave an organization inadequately prepared to handle violent incidents should they occur. A proactive stance on work-related violence can prevent damage to property, lost productivity, and even possible tragedy.

An essential component of the intervention process with respect to violence is professional support. By enlisting the support of services such as employee assistance programs through human resources departments or outside assessment professionals, potentially violent behaviour can be recognized and effectively managed.

When Personalities Collide

Disagreement about ideas can promote innovation and creativity, but disagreement between people on a personal level leads to demoralization, stress, and low productivity. As the supervisor, you'll be called upon to help resolve confrontations between the members of your group.

Here are a few suggestions:

Assess the Situation

- How serious is the disagreement?

- Is it negatively impacting the project or the team's productivity?

- Are your members able to effectively solve the problem themselves within a suitable time frame? If they can, encourage them to do so. This will foster a sense of personal responsibility.

- Encourage listening by the parties involved so that they understand each other's point of view. Get them to focus on common goals and interests.

- Follow up to verify progress. *You should point out that you view the conflict as an obstacle for the workgroup as a whole, and emphasize the need for a mutually agreeable solution.*

Inform the individuals that if they cannot resolve their differences within an agreed upon time frame, you will be obliged to mediate the situation.

Arrange a Mediation Meeting (If the parties cannot resolve the issues themselves)

- ▶ The meeting should be held in a neutral place.

- ▶ Arrange the meeting room with both parties facing you rather than each other.

- ▶ Start the meeting as soon as both parties arrive and inform them on how you intend to run the meeting. Be sure they agree on the process.

- ▶ Establish the ground rules. Participants must genuinely try to understand each other's points of view, stick with facts rather than engaging in personal confrontations, show respect for one another by not speaking over each other, and be open to compromise.

- ▶ Emphasize that your role is that of a neutral mediator and explain the consequences to the workgroup and the parties in conflict if the disagreement is not resolved.

- ▶ Let the participants state their positions in turn, without interruption. You may want to record these on a flip chart. At the end of each statement, recap the major points on the flip chart, being certain that everyone agrees with and understands the premises.

▸ You should now have each party summarize the position of the other party. Have them identify the key issues. Be sure these issues are based on fact and are not of a personal nature. Review and summarize the main issues and ask the individuals to confirm their understanding.

▸ First, seek suggestions for resolution from the people involved. If there are no suggestions forthcoming, offer some of your own.

▸ Record the suggested solutions next to the issues they address. Seek clear-cut suggestions as to how these solutions could be implemented and specific dates by which you would see results. Get everybody's agreement on these solutions and dates.

SUPERVISOR TIP

Whenever a mediation meeting is necessary, establish the ground rules. Participants must genuinely try to understand each other's points of view, stick with facts rather than engaging in personal confrontations, show respect for one another by not speaking over each other, and be open to compromise.

▸ If appropriate, praise the individuals on their honesty and openness.

▸ Prepare a memo outlining the issues, solutions, actions, and dates, and circulate it to the people involved. You should make it clear to everyone that you are monitoring the conflict.

▶ Follow up. Arrange another meeting within a reasonably brief period of time to review progress. Compliment the parties if they are implementing the solutions discussed to resolve the conflict and reassure them that you are available in a supporting role.

If, on the other hand, no progress has been made, determine why and let the parties know, in no uncertain terms, the consequences of not resolving the issue.

It is essential to remember in the course of resolving a disagreement, that if you have any reason to believe an upset or angry employee could hurt you or others, immediately summon help. Anger that turns to violence is no longer a resolvable short-term problem. Never go into a room alone with someone you suspect could become violent.

Many organizations now have specific policies in place for dealing with potentially violent situations. Be sure to familiarize yourself with these policies.